KT-167-264

NEWARK & SHERWOOD COLLEGE L.C.

0045263X

Lincoln College

1071518

The
Gentleman &
Cabinet-Maker's
Director

THOMAS CHIPPENDALE

The Gentleman & Cabinet-Maker's Director

Reprint of the Third Edition
With a Biographical Sketch
and Photographic Supplement
of Chippendale-Type
Furniture

DOVER PUBLICATIONS, INC.
NEW YORK

NEWARK & SHERWOOD COLLEGE
LEARNING CENTRE

CENTRE	Newark
CHECKED	TRD.
ZONE	Grey
ZONE MARK / SUFFIX	684.1 CHI
LOAN PERIOD	1 month.

Copyright © 1966 by Dover Publications, Inc.
All rights reserved under Pan American and International
Copyright Conventions.

This Dover edition, first published in 1966, is an unabridged
and unaltered republication of the third edition published by
the author in London in 1762. This edition also contains
a biographical sketch of Thomas Chippendale by N. I. Bienenstock (Editor, *The Furniture World*) and a photographic
supplement showing various styles of Chippendale-type
furniture.

International Standard Book Number: 0-486-21601-2
Library of Congress Catalog Card Number: 66-24135

Manufactured in the United States of America
Dover Publications, Inc.
31 East 2nd Street, Mineola, N.Y. 11501

T H E

GENTLEMAN and CABINET-MAKER's
D I R E C T O R:

Being a large COLLECTION of the

Moſt ELEGANT and USEFUL DESIGNS

O F

HOUSEHOLD FURNITURE,

In the Moſt FASHIONABLE TASTE.

Including a great VARIETY of

CHAIRS, SOFAS, BEDS, and COUCHES; CHINA-TABLES, DRESSING-TABLES, SHAVING-TABLES, BASON-STANDS, and TEAKETTLE-STANDS; FRAMES for MARBLE-SLABS, BUREAU-DRESSING-TABLES, and COMMODES; WRITING-TABLES, and LIBRARY-TABLES; LIBRARY-BOOK-CASES, ORGAN-CASES for private Rooms, or Churches, DESKS, and BOOK-CASES; DRESSING and WRITING-TABLES with BOOK-CASES, TOILETS, CABINETS, and CLOATHS-PRESSES; CHINA-CASES, CHINA-SHELVES, and BOOK-SHELVES; CANDLE-STANDS, TERMS for BUSTS, STANDS for CHINA JARS, and PEDESTALS; CISTERNS for WATER, LANTHORNS, and CHANDELIERS; FIRE-SCREENS, BRACKETS, and CLOCK-CASES; PIER-GLASSES, and TABLE-FRAMES; GIRANDOLES, CHIMNEY-PIECES, and PICTURE-FRAMES; STOVE-GRATES, BOARDERS, FRETS, CHINESE-RAILING, and BRASS-WORK, for Furniture.

AND OTHER

O R N A M E N T S.

TO WHICH IS PREFIXED,

A Short EXPLANATION of the Five ORDERS of ARCHITECTURE;

WITH

Proper DIRECTIONS for executing the moſt difficult Pieces, the Mouldings being exhibited at large, and the Dimenſions of each DESIGN ſpecified.

The Whole comprehended in TWO HUNDRED COPPER-PLATES, neatly engraved.

Calculated to improve and refine the preſent TASTE, and ſuited to the Fancy and Circumſtances of Perſons in all Degrees of Life.

By THOMAS CHIPPENDALE,

CABINET-MAKER and UPHOLSTERER, in St. Martin's Lane, London.

THE THIRD EDITION.

L O N D O N:

Printed for the AUTHOR, and ſold at his Houſe, in St. Martin's Lane; Alſo by T. BECKET and P. A. DE HONDT, in the Strand.
MDCCLXII.

P R E F A C E.

OF all the ARTS which are either improved or ornamented by Architecture, that of CABINET-MAKING is not only the moſt uſeful and ornamental, but capable of receiving as great Aſſiſtance from it as any whatever. I have there-fore prefixed to the following Deſigns a ſhort Explanation of the Five Orders. Without an Acquaintance with this Science, and ſome Knowledge of the Rules of Perſpective, the Cabinet-Maker cannot make the Deſigns of his Work intelligible, nor ſhew, in a little Compaſs, the whole Conduct and Effect of the Piece. Theſe, therefore, ought to be carefully ſtudied by every one who would excel in this Branch, ſince they are the very Soul and Baſis of his Art.

THE Title-Page has already called the following Work, *The Gentleman and Cabinet-Maker's Director*, as being calculated to aſſiſt the one in the Choice, and the other in the Execution of the Deſigns; which are ſo contrived, that if no one Drawing ſhould ſingly anſwer the Gentleman's Taſte, there will yet be found a Variety of Hints, ſufficient to conſtruct a new one.

I HAVE been encouraged to begin and carry on this Work not only by Perſons of Diſtinction, but of eminent Taſte for Performances of this Sort; who have, upon many Occaſions, ſignified ſome Surprize and Regret, that an Art capable of ſo much Perfection and Refinement, ſhould be executed with ſo little Propriety and Elegance. How far the following Sheets may remove a Complaint, which I am afraid is not altogether groundleſs, the judicious Reader will determine: I hope, however, the Novelty, as well as the Uſefulneſs of the Performance, will make ſome Atonement for its Faults and Imperfections. I am ſenſible, there are too many to be found in it; for I frankly confeſs, that in executing many of the Drawings, my Pencil has but faintly copied out thoſe Images that my Fancy ſuggeſted; and had they not been publiſhed till I could have pronounced them perfect, perhaps they had never ſeen the Light. Nevertheleſs, I was not upon that Account afraid to let them go abroad, for I have been told, that the greateſt Maſters of every other Art have laboured under the ſame Difficulty.

I AM not afraid of the Fate an Author uſually meets with on his firſt Appearance from a Set of Criticks who are never wanting to ſhew their Wit and Malice on the Performances of others: I ſhall repay their Cenſures with Contempt. Let them unmoleſted deal out their pointleſs Abuſe, and convince the World they have neither Good-nature to commend, Judgment to correct, nor Skill to execute what they find Fault with.

THE

P R E F A C E.

THE Correction of the Judicious and Impartial I shall always receive with Diffidence in my own Abilities, and Respect to theirs. But though the following Designs were more perfect than my Fondness for my own Offspring could ever suppose them, I should yet be far from expecting the united Approbation of ALL those whose Sentiments have an undoubted Claim to be regarded; for a thousand accidental Circumstances may concur in dividing the Opinions of the most improved Judges, and the most unprejudiced will find it difficult to disengage himself from a partial Affection to some particular Beauties, of which the general Course of his Studies, or the peculiar Cast of his Temper may have rendered him most sensible. The Mind, when pronouncing Judgment upon any Work of Taste and Genius, is apt to decide of its Merit according as those Circumstances which she most admires either prevail, or are deficient.

UPON the whole, I have here given no Design but what may be executed with Advantage by the Hands of a skilful Workman, though some of the Profession have been diligent enough to represent them (especially those after the Gothick and Chinese Manner) as so many specious Drawings, impossible to be worked off by any Mechanick whatsoever. I will not scruple to attribute this to Malice, Ignorance, and Inability; and I am confident I can convince all Noblemen, Gentlemen, or others, who will honour me with their Commands, that every Design in the Book can be improved, both as to Beauty and Enrichment, in the Execution of it, by

Their Most Obedient Servant,

St. Martin's Lane,
Feb. 27, 1762.

THOMAS CHIPPENDALE.

THE

GENERAL PROPORTIONS
OF THE
TUSCAN ORDER.
PLATE I.

TAKE any Height propofed for this Order, and divide it into five equal Parts; one of thofe Parts fhall be the Height of the Pedeftal according to the fmall Divifion of the Scale, on the left Hand; the other four Parts above muft be divided into five Parts, according to the outmoft Line on the left Hand; the upper fifth part fhall be the Height of the Entablature, and the other four Parts betwixt the Pedeftal and Entablature, fhall be the Height of the Column, including its Bafe and Capital : and this Height being divided into feven Parts, one of thofe Parts will be the Diameter of the Column, which Diameter is divided into fixty equal Parts, and is called a Module; and this will ferve to fet off all the Mouldings for this Order. You have all the Particulars of the Mouldings at large on the right Hand; the Bafe and Capital are each in Height a Semi-diameter of the Column; the Column muft be divided into three equal Parts betwixt the Capital and Bafe, and from the top of the lower Divifion it is diminifhed one-fifth of its Semi-diameter on each Side. The Method of diminifhing the Column is explained in the middle Scheme; the Breadth of the Die of the Pedeftal is determined by the Projection of the Bafe of the Column.

THE

GENERAL PROPORTIONS
OF THE
DORICK ORDER.
PLATE II.

TAKE any Height upon a ftraight Line, as in the TUSCAN Order, and divide it into five equal Parts; one of them fhall be the Height of the Pedeftal; the other four Parts muft be divided into five Parts, one of which is the Height of the Entablature; the remaining four Parts muft be divided into eight Parts; one of them is the Diameter of the Column, or Module, which divide into fixty equal Parts, as in the TUSCAN Order, to fet off all the Mouldings, as you will fee on the right Hand, where you have the Plan of the Cornice. The Column diminifhes one-fixth of its Semi-diameter on each Side, from one-third Part of its Height, to the Top of the Capital. The Bafe and Capital are each in Height a Semi-diameter.

THE

GENERAL PROPORTIONS
OF THE
IONICK ORDER.
PLATE III.

TAKE any Height, as in the foregoing Orders, and divide it into five equal Parts, one of thefe Parts is the Height of the Pedeftal; the other four being divided into fix Parts, one of them is the Height of the Entablature; the remaining five Parts muft be divided into nine equal Parts; one of them is the Diameter of the Column or Module, which is divided into fixty equal Parts as before; the Mouldings are at large, with a Scale or Module to draw them. The Column is diminifhed one-fixth of its Semi-diameter on each Side, from one-third Part of its Height. The Bafe and Capital are each in Height a Semi-diameter.

THE

THE

GENERAL PROPORTIONS

OF THE

CORINTHIAN ORDER.

PLATE IV.

THE whole Height is divided into five Parts, one of them muſt be for the Pedeſtal, the other four remaining Parts muſt be divided into ſix; one of them will give the Height of the Entablature, the other five, betwixt the Pedeſtal and Entablature, muſt be divided into ten Parts, one of which is the Diameter of the Column, or Module, which divide into ſixty equal Parts as before; the Baſe is in Height a Semi-diameter of the Column; the Capital is one Module, and ten Parts, in Height: The other Dimenſions are as in the IONICK Order.

THE

GENERAL PROPORTIONS

OF THE

COMPOSITE ORDER.

PLATE V.

TAKE any determined Height, as in the CORINTHIAN Order, and divide it into five Parts, one Part ſhall be the Height of the Pedeſtal, the other four Parts muſt be divided again into ſix Parts as before; one of them is the Height of the Entablature: The Height of the Capital is one Module, and ten Parts: The Column diminiſhes one-ſixth of its Semi-diameter on each Side, from one-third Part of the Height. The Dimenſions are as in the CORINTHIAN Order.

THE

B A S E S

FOR THE

COLUMNS of each ORDER.

PLATE VI.

THE Baſes are in Height a Semi-diameter of the Column; their Projections are one-third of the Height; their Members are of an eaſy Form, being moſt of them a Semi-circular, except the Scotia, which is a Mixti-linear drawn from two Centers, in this Manner, as in the IONICK Baſe. Having drawn and divided the Bigneſs of each Member, and the Centers of the upper and lower Torus, then let fall a Perpendicular from the Center of the upper Torus, and divide it within the Space of the Scotia into ſeven Parts, the three uppermoſt will be the Segment of the Circle drawn to the oblique Line: The other Segment is drawn by fixing the Center where the Oblique cuts the Perpendicular; the other Scotias are drawn in the ſame Manner. The Mouldings are all the ſame as pricked or marked in the Orders.

THE

B A S E S and C A P S

OF THE

PEDESTALS of each ORDER.

PLATE VII.

THE Projection of the Baſe of the Pedeſtal is equal to its Height, and the Caps project the ſame; the Mouldings are pricked off as they are drawn in the Order before.

A RULE

A

RULE for DRAWING

THE

SPIRAL LINES of the VOLUTE

OF THE

IONICK ORDER.

PLATE VIII.

TAKE your Compaſſes, and extend from 1 in the Eye of the Volute, to the greateſt Extent, and ſweep with them a Quarter of a Circle; then holding ſtill in the Point where the Compaſſes ended the Quarter Circle, bring the other Point of the Compaſſes to 2, in the Eye of the Volute; there ſweep another Quarter of a Circle, ſtill holding your Compaſſes in that Point; bring the other Point of your Compaſſes to 3 in the Eye of the Volute, and ſweep another Quarter of a Circle; then hold your Compaſſes in that Point, and bring the other Point of your Compaſſes to 4 in the Eye of the Volute, then ſweep the other Quarter: ſo by this Means you will complete one Round of the Volute. Then proceed in the ſame Manner from 4, to 5, 6, 7, and ſo on to 12. Take Notice of the Eye of the Volute at large, and obſerve to divide each Diviſion into three equal Parts, as is done betwixt 2 and 6, and let the Point of your Compaſs be placed in the Points *c, d, f,* &c. to diminiſh the Fillet of the Volute.

PLATES IX. X. XI. XII. XIII. XIV.

Are various Deſigns of Chairs for Patterns. The front Feet are moſtly different, for the greater Choice. Care muſt be taken in drawing them at large. The Seats look beſt when ſtuffed over the Rails, and have a Braſs Border neatly chaſed; but are moſt commonly done with Braſs Nails, in one or two Rows; and ſometimes the Nails are done to imitate Fretwork. They are uſually covered with the ſame Stuff as the Window-Curtains. The Height of the Back ſeldom exceeds twenty-two Inches above the Seats: The other Dimenſions are in Plate IX. Sometimes the Dimenſions are leſs, to ſuit the Chairs to the Rooms.

PLATE XV.

Three Deſigns of Chairs with Ribband-Backs. Several Sets have been made, which have given entire Satisfaction. If any of the ſmall Ornaments ſhould be thought ſuperfluous, they may be left out, without ſpoiling the Deſign. If the Seats are covered with red Morocco, they will have a fine Effect.

PLATE XVI.

Six Deſigns for Backs of Chairs.

PLATES XVII. XVIII.

Six Deſigns of Chairs for Halls, Paſſages, or Summer-Houſes. They may be made either of Mahogony, or any other Wood, and painted, and have commonly wooden Seats. If the Carving of the Chairs in Plate XVIII. was thought ſuperfluous, the Outlines may be preſerved, and they will look very well. The Height of the Gothick Back is two Feet, four Inches, and the others one Foot, eleven Inches, and the Height of the Seat ſeventeen or eighteen Inches. If you divide the Height of the Backs in the Number of Inches given, you will have a Meaſure to take off of the Breadth of the circular Parts of each Back. Arms, if required, may be put to thoſe Chairs.

PLATE XIX.

Two Deſigns of French Chairs with Elbows, and for the greater Variety, the Feet and Elbows are different. The little Moulding, round the Bottom of the Edge of the Rails, has a good
Effect

Effect. The Backs and Seats are stuffed, and covered with Spanish Leather, or Damask, &c. and nailed with Brass Nails. The Seat is twenty-seven Inches wide in Front, twenty-two Inches from the Front to the Back, and twenty-three Inches wide behind; the Height of the Back is twenty-five Inches, and the Height of the Seat fourteen Inches and an Half, including Casters.

PLATES XX. XXI. XXII. XXIII.

Eight Designs of French Chairs, which may be executed to Advantage. Some of them are intended to be open below at the Back: which make them very light, without having a bad Effect. The Dimensions are the same as in Plate XIX. only that the highest Part of the Back is two Feet, five Inches: But sometimes these Dimensions vary, according to the Bigness of the Rooms they are intended for. A skilful Workman may also lessen the Carving, without any Prejudice to the Design. Both the Backs and Seats must be covered with Tapestry, or other sort of Needlework.

PLATE XXIV.

Two Designs of Chairs for Gardens, and a long Seat. That marked A, is proper for Arbours, or Summer-Houses, and C proper for Grottos; the Seat marked B, may be placed in Walks, or at the Ends of Avenues. The Backs may be cut out of the solid Board, and fixed to the Back Edges of the Seats. The Dimensions are as in Plate XVII. or XVIII. The Length of Seat B is seven Feet.

PLATE XXV.

Three Designs of Chairs. That in the Middle is proper for a Library; the two others are Gothick, and fit for Eating-Parlours; the Dimensions as in Plates IX. and X.

PLATES XXVI. XXVII. and XXVIII.

Nine Designs of Chairs after the Chinese Manner, and are very proper for a Lady's Dressing-Room: especially if it is hung with India Paper. They will likewise suit Chinese Temples. They have commonly Cane-Bottoms, with loose Cushions; but, if required, may have stuffed Seats, and Brass Nails.

PLATES XXIX. and XXX.

Four Designs of Sofas. When made large, they have a Bolster and Pillow at each End, and Cushions at the Back, which may be laid down occasionally, and form a Mattrass. The upper Sofa, in Plate XXIX. is designed to have the Back-Corners circular, which must look well. The Sizes differ greatly; but commonly they are from six to nine, or ten feet long; the Depth of the Seat, from Front to Back, from two Feet, three Inches, to three Feet; and the Height of the Seat one Foot, two Inches, with Casters. The Scrolls are eighteen or nineteen Inches high. Part of the Carving may be left out, if required.

PLATE XXXI.

A Design of a Sofa for a grand Apartment, and will require great Care in the Execution, to make the several Parts come in such a Manner, that all the Ornaments join without the least Fault: and if the Embossments all along are rightly managed, and gilt with burnished Gold, the whole will have a noble Appearance. The Carving at the Top is the Emblem of Watchfulness, Assiduity, and Rest. The Pillows and Cushions must not be omitted, though they are not in the Design. The Dimensions are nine Feet long, without the Scrolls; the broadest Part of the Seat, from Front to Back, two Feet, six Inches; the Height of the Back from the Seat, three Feet, six Inches; and the Height of the Seat one Foot, two Inches, without Casters. I would advise the Workman to make a Model of it at large, before he begins to execute it.

PLATE XXXII.

Two Designs of Couches, or what the French call *Péché Mortel*. They are sometimes made to take asunder in the Middle; one Part makes a large Easy-Chair, and the other a

Stool,

Stool, and the Feet join in the Middle, which looks badly: Therefore I would recommend their being made, as in thefe Defigns, with a pretty thick Mattrafs. The Dimenfions are fix Feet long in the Clear, and two Feet, fix Inches, to three Feet-broad.

PLATE XXXIII.

A Defign of a Sofa with a Chinefe Canopy, with Curtains and Valences tied up in Drapery, and may be converted into a Bed, by making the front Part of the Seat to draw forward, and the Sides made to fold and turn in with ftrong Iron Hinges, and a proper Stretcher to keep out and fupport the Sides when open. The Curtains muft be likewife made to come forward, and when let down will form a Tent. A, is the Lath of the Curtain; B, Half of the Plan of the Canopy; C, the Profile of the Wood-Work; D, an Ornament that goes round the Infide; E, the Shell-work at the Bottom of the Canopy.

PLATES XXXIV. XXXV.

Ten Defigns of Bed-Pillars. A, B, C, D, E, in Plate XXXIV. are Gothick; *b* is the Plan of the Pillar B, and the Pedeftal Part; *c* is the Plan of C; *d* the Plan of D; and *e* of E. A Scale is annexed. No Length can be fixed, as that will be determined by the Height of the Room they are for. They are all defigned with Pedeftals, which muft certainly look better than Bafes of Stuff round the Bed, and the Pillars feem to be unfupported. The Defigns are very clear, and need no farther Explanation.

PLATES XXXVI. XXXVII.

Seven Defigns of Cornices, for Beds, or Windows: They muft look well, if they are rightly executed.

PLATE XXXVIII.

A Defign of a Bed, with carved Cornices, which may be gilt, or covered with the fame Stuff as the Curtains. Thefe are omitted, but may be made either to draw up in Drapery, or to run on a Rod, as may be feen in fome of the other Beds. The Sweep at the Top of the Tefter is Half of a flat Ellipfis, as at *b*. A is the Lath *a*; B is the Corner-Rib, which goes from Corner to Corner, croffing in the Middle. C is the Rib which goes from the Middle of the Lath, *a*; which Sweep is got by the Interfection of Lines, as at B. D is the Moulding which goes round the Infide of the Tefter. The Cornice muft rife as high as it can, to hide the Top of the Tefter. The Bed-Pillars have Pedeftals, and the Bafes are fitted between.

PLATE XXXIX.

A Bed which has been made for the Earls of Dumfries and Morton. One of the Pillars is compofed of Reeds, with a Palm-Branch twifting round. The Tefter is covered, and the Bottom-Edge of the Cove is cut into the Shape nearly that of the Cornice, and a thin, flight Ornament fixed on, and the Infide Valens fixed to it. In the Middle of the Tefter is a carved, oval Ornament, three Feet, nine Inches, by two Feet, eight Inches; and from that to each Corner, is a Piece of Foliage and Flowerings. The Corner-Pieces, which come down from the Cornice, are Wood, and the Valens fixed to them. The Pillars are eight Feet, fix Inches high, and the Bedftead fix Feet, feven Inches long, and fix Feet wide.

PLATE XL.

A Defign of a Bed, with a Plan and Section of the Tefter. D, A, C, is the Section, and D, B, C, Half of the Plan. The pricked Lines that fall from the Section, give the Lines for the oval Cove in the Plan. The Curtains may be made either to be tied up in Drapery, or to draw on a Rod: The Pedeftals look better uncovered. The Dimenfions as in Plate XXXIX.

PLATE XLI.

A Defign of a Bed, with the proper Dimenfions, and requires no Explanation. B is another Cornice, which may be covered with the fame Stuff as the Curtains. *a, a, a,* are the Lath, with Pullies to draw up the Curtains.

PLATE

P L A T E   XLII.

A Defign of a Canopy-Bed, with its Head-Board. Both the Curtains and Valences are to draw up in Drapery. The Dimenfions are fpecified: *a* is a fourth Part of the Tefter; *c* is a fmall oval Dome in the Infide; *b, d,* the outfide Canopy; *h, h,* a Mofaick Work in the Flat round the Dome; *i* is the Lath which goes round the Bed; *f* is the Bed-Pillars; *k, k, k,* the Places where the Pullies are fixed to draw up the Curtains.

P L A T E   XLIII.

A Defign of a Dome-Bed. The Bottom-Edge of the Dome, or Lath, *g,* is the Half of a flat Ellipfis. A, A, A, are the Lath which the Dome is fixed to, and made into the Shape of the Lath, *g,* which the Cornice is fixed to. B is the Quarter of the Dome, with Ornaments in the Center and Corners; C is the other Quarter; *e, e, e,* the Ribs which form the Dome; *o, o, o,* the Length of the Line *p, p;* the double Lines at *b,* are the Section of the Dome from Corner to Corner; the Spaces between the Ribs, *e, e, e,* may be filled with light dry Wood; *l* is a Block in the Center, to fix the Ends of the Ribs in; *m, m,* the Plan of the Bed-Pillars; *f* is the Plan of the Rib, which cuts the Dome through from Side to Side; the Spaces, *i, i,* and *k, k,* where the Rib *f* is, muft be divided in the fame Manner, as K, K, and K, K, at *b,* by which Means, the Sweeps of all the other Ribs, *e, e, e,* may be got, which form the Dome, C; *p, q,* is the fame Height as P, Q; *n* is the dotted Line which cuts the Dome from Corner to Corner; *r, r, r,* the Pullies for the Lines to draw up the Curtains; S is another Cornice. A Scale is annexed, to take off the Dimenfions of the Plan and Profile. The Bedftead is fix Feet wide, fix Feet, feven Inches long, and one Foot high; and the whole Height without the Vafe, is ten Feet, four Inches, and the Vafe itfelf eighteen or twenty Inches.

P L A T E   XLIV.

A Defign of a Gothick Bed, with a flat Tefter. The Cornice will look very well, if rightly executed. A, is the Lath; *c, c, c,* the Pullies where the Lines are fixed to draw up the Curtains; B is an Ornament, made of Lace or Binding, for the Tefter.

P L A T E   XLV.

A Defign of a Bed. The Feet-Pillars and Corners of the Cornice are different. The Head-Part of the Bed muft be in the fame Shape, all the Way up to the Canopy, as the Foot-Rail and Foot-Cornice, and continued in the Canopy to the upper Work, which goes round the top Part of it. The flat Part of the Canopy in the Infide muft be pannelled, and a carved Ornament go round it. The Pillars ftand with the Angles forward, which give an Advantage for the better finifhing of the Corners of the Cornice, and the Ornaments which go up each Corner of the Canopy. The Lath of the Tefter muft have the fame Shape as the Plan of the Pedeftal-Part of the Bedftead. The Sides of the Bed run ftreight.

P L A T E   XLVI.

A Defign of a Couch-Bed, with a Canopy. The Curtains muft be made to draw up in Feftoon, with Pullies properly fixed to the Pillars. *e* is a Brafs Rod which fupports the Canopy; G is the Lath which fixes on the Top of the Pillar; F, the Canopy; D, in the Plan, is the Line D above; E, E, is the Line *e, e,* above; *c, c,* the Shape of the Lath of the Canopy; K is a Projection where the Ornament is fixed on, which goes up each Corner of the crooked Part of the Pillar, and is fixed on after the Furniture is put on; H is the Moulding, carved in Strapwork, or Shellwork, to go round the Canopy. The Dimenfions are fix Feet, eight Inches long, and five Feet broad; but there is no Neceffity for its being fo broad.

N. B. This Couch was made for an Alcove in Lord Pembroke's Houfe, at Whitehall.

P L A T E   XLVII.

A Defign of a State-Bed, which I fubmit to the Judicious and Candid, for their Approbation. There are found Magnificence, Proportion, and Harmony. If the Pedeftals of the Bedftead, the Pillars, Cornice, and Top of the Dome, are gilt with burnifhed Gold, and the Furniture is fuitable, the whole will look extremely grand, and be fit for the moft ftately Apartment. The ingenious Artift may alfo, in the Execution, give full Scope to his Capacity. The

Bedftead

Bedftead fhould be fix or feven Feet broad, feven or eight Feet long, and the whole Height fourteen or fifteen Feet. A Workman of Genius will eafily comprehend the Defign : But I would advife him, in order to prevent Miftakes, to make firft a Model of the fame at large; which will fave both Time and Expence.

PLATE XLVIII.

A Defign of a Gothick Bed, with Drapery Curtains. The Pillars are made into eight Cants, and indented. B is a fourth of the Tefter; *a, a*, the fame Length as A, A, above, in the Section, which goes from Corner to Corner, to form the Roof, and then you have the Corner-Hips formed. Divide the Length, A, A, as you fee it, and then raife two Perpendiculars up to B, and divide that Length into the fame Number of Divifions as below, which give the Sweep of the Ribs, *c, c, c*. The Curtains are drawn by Lines on each Side of the Bed, as may be feen, by Pullies being fixed at the Corners. The other Parts require no Explanation.

PLATE XLIX.

Four Defigns of Tent, or Field-Beds, A, B, C, D. That marked A hath a Canopy, which begins to form itfelf at *e, e*, with four Ribs, which fix into a Lath at *f.* The Dome may be omitted, and four Vafes put in at the Corners of the Canopy, which is made into eight or ten Cants.

The Furniture of all thefe Bedfteads is made to take off, and the Laths are hung with Hinges, for Convenience of folding up.

The Bed at C. The Laths which form the Tefter are ftreight in Front, and are made into the Shape of the Ornament the other Way. In the Center is a Canopy, with eight or ten Ribs, (made to take out) and fixed into a feparate Lath.

The Beds D and B have no Canopies, and are made in the fame Manner as the other two.

PLATE L.

A Couch with a Canopy. The Curtains muft be made to draw up in Drapery, and to let down, when it is occafionally converted into a Bed. This Sort of Couches is very fit for Alcoves, or fuch deep Receffes as are often feen in large Apartments. It may alfo be placed at the End of a long Gallery. If the Curtains and Valences are adorned with large Gold Fringes and Taffels, and the Ornaments gilt with burnifhed Gold, it will look very grand. The Crane, at the Top of the Canopy, is the Emblem of Care and Watchfulnefs : which, I think, is not unbecoming a Place of Reft. The Length of the Bed cannot be lefs than fix Feet in the Clear, but may be more, if required. The Breadth is three Feet, or more, in Proportion to the Length, The Height muft be determined by the Place it is to ftand in.

PLATE LI.

Two Defigns of Tables for holding each a Set of China, and may be ufed as Tea-Tables. A, A, are Half of the Plans of the Tops. C is an Ornament to go between the Feet. Thofe Tables look very well, when rightly executed.

PLATE LII.

A Defign of a Dreffing-Table for a Lady; the Drawer above the Recefs hath all Conveniences for Dreffing, and the Top of it is a Dreffing-Glafs, which comes forward with folding Hinges. On each Side is a Cupboard, with Glafs Doors, which may be either tranfparent or filvered ; and in the Infide, Drawers, or Pigeon-Holes. Two Dreffing-Tables have been made of Rofe-Wood, from this Defign, which gave an entire Satisfaction: All the Ornaments were gilt. B is the Plan of the under Part; A, A, the Plan of the Cupboards; C the Plan of the Dreffing-Drawer; *d, d*, a Glafs made to rife, and hung with Hinges; *f, f*, Places for Combs, Rings, Bottles, Boxes, &c. The Dimenfions are fixed to the Defign.

PLATE

PLATE LIII.

Two Defigns of Breakfaft-Tables. One hath a Stretching-Rail, and the Feet are canted and funk in. The other hath a Shelf, inclofed with Fretwork: Sometimes they are inclofed with Brafs Wirework. In the Front is a Recefs for the Knees, &c.

PLATE LIV.

A Defign of a Shaving-Table, with a folding Top, and a Glafs to rife out with a Spring-Catch. A, A, are Places for holding Soap and other Neceflaries, and behind them are Places for Razors; B, B, Places for Bottles; D is a Scheme to bring the Glafs forward, when a Gentleman is fhaving; g is the Glafs brought forward, with a Brafs Frame; f, f, f, is the Joints as it is hung; C is a fmall Piece of Brafs, which flides up and down in a Groove, as may be feen by the dotted Line. The Dimenfions are fixed.

The other is the Defign of a Bafon-Stand, with a Glafs to rife, as the Shaving-Table.

PLATE LV.

Three Defigns of Bafon-Stands, and three Tea-kettle-Stands. The Bafon-Stand in the Middle hath four Feet, and four Gothick Pillars, and an Arch on each Side. The others are fo eafy to underftand, that they want no Explanation.

PLATES LVI. LVII.

Two Defigns of Side-Boards, with their Dimenfions; but thefe vary according to the Bignefs of the Rooms they ftand in. The Mouldings are at large.

PLATES LVIII. LIX:

Two Side-Boards, as above. The Feet and Rails of Plate LIX. are cut through; which gives it an airy Look; but will be too flight for Marble-Tops: Therefore the Tops will be better made of Wood. Plate LVIII. hath different Feet, for the greater Choice: The Mouldings as in Plates LVI. and LVII.

PLATE LX.

A Gothick Side-Board, with different Feet, one cut through, the other folid. A is the Square of the folid Foot; b, b, the Rails mortifed into the Foot A; g is the Plan of the Moulding g; F, e, the Moulding for the Top, drawn round the two front Columns, F, e, in the Plan; D the Moulding in the Plan D, which goes round the Frame; e is the fmall Aftragal, which is turned upon the Columns.

PLATE LXI.

Two Side-Boards, with different Feet. B is the Plan of the Table above it; A, A, A, is where the Feet are placed; c, c, c, the Mouldings at large, drawn to an Inch Scale.

PLATE LXII.

Two Defigns of Commode-Bureau-Tables, with their Plans below, and proper Scales. The upper Drawer may be of the whole Length of the Table, and have the fame Divifions as C of Plate LII. The Recefs for the Knees is of a circular Form, which looks more handfome than when it it is quite ftreight.

PLATE LXIII.

Two Bureau-Dreffing-Tables. The upper Drawers may be divided in like Manner as at C, Plate LII. The ornamental Parts are intended for Brafs-Work, which I would advife fhould be modelled in Wax, and then caft from thefe Models. The under Parts may be made into Drawers inftead of Cupboards. The Dimenfions are fpecified.

PLATE

PLATE LXIV.

A Commode-Table, with a Scale and Dimensions. A is Half the Plan; B is the Upright of the Table.

PLATE LXV.

A Commode-Table. A is the Plan of the Top with a Scale of the Dimensions. It will have a very good Effect, if well executed: The Ornaments may be omitted in the upper Drawer, if required.

PLATE LXVI.

A Commode-Table. A is Half of the Plan. B is the Upright of the Table. C is the Mouldings of the Top, with a Scale to take off the Dimensions.

PLATE LXVII.

Two Commode-Tables. That in the Right is all Drawers in Front; the upper one may be a Dressing-Drawer, and of the whole Length of the Table. The ornamental Parts are carved out of Wood. That on the Left may be divided into nine Drawers, or have only three of the whole Length of the Table. The Dimensions are specified: The Ornaments may be of Brass, if required.

PLATE LXVIII.

Two Commode-Tables. That on the Left is drawn in Perspective: The Ornaments may be Brass; the Middle is a Door, with a Drawer above, and Drawers at each End. That on the Right hath two Doors, which represent Drawers, and a long Drawer above: The Pilasters at the Ends must be fixed to the Doors, and open with them. The Plan is below, with a Scale.

PLATE LXIX.

A Commode-Table, with Drawers at Top and in the Middle, and Doors at the Ends. The Ornaments should be carved very light: The Terms for the Corners are different. A is Half the Plan. B the Upright of the Work, and a Scale for the Dimensions.

PLATE LXX.

Two Commode-Tables. That on the Right hath Doors, and may have sliding Shelves within for Cloaths: The Ornaments on the Corners, and at the Bottom of the Doors, may open with the Doors. That on the Left may have either Drawers, or Doors, at the Ends.

PLATE LXXI.

A Commode. The Bass Relief in the Middle may be carved in Wood, or cast in Brass, or painted on Wood or Copper. That Part in the Middle may be a Door, with the Ornaments on it, and the End Parts in the same Manner. On the Top of the Commode is a Design of a Sur-tout, to be made in Silver: A Candlestand at each End is very proper. I would advise to model this Design before Execution, as it will save Time, and prevent Mistakes.

PLATE LXXII.

A Writing-Table, with Drawers in the under Part. In the Middle of the upper Part are small Drawers, and Pigeon-Holes, and a Place for Books. A is the Plan of the upper Part; B the Plan of the under Part; C the Cornice; D and E the upper and lower Mouldings of the upper Part. The Dimensions are specified.

PLATE LXXIII.

A Writing-Table. Half of the front Feet come out with the Drawer, which parts at *b*, *b*. A is the Plan of the Table, with the Partitions; *g* is a quadrant Drawer, for Ink and Sand. D is

the

the Profile of the Side of the Drawer; B, B, the Plan of the front Feet; *c, c*, the Mouldings which go round; *f, f*, the Projection of the Top of the Table.

PLATE LXXIV.

A Writing-Table, as LXXIII. A is the Plan of the Table; B the Flap which rises to write upon; C, B, the Slider that slides, as in the Profile *f, f*; D, D, the Drawers at the Ends; E, the Profile of the Table.

PLATE LXXV.

A Writing-Table. The Doors at the Ends may go up to the Top, and have upright, sliding Partitions for Books, or Drawers, within. The middle Drawer need be no longer than the Opening of the middle Part, and must be made into a Writing-Drawer. The upper Part hath two Doors; the Inside is divided into Pigeon-Holes, with Labels of the Alphabet over them, and Drawers on each End. The Mouldings are at large, and a Scale. On the left Hand is a different Design of an under Part.

PLATE LXXVI.

A Writing-Table in the Gothick Taste. The middle Part hath a Recefs for the Knees, as may be seen by the Plan B. The Pillars are fixed to the Doors, and open with them. A is the whole Plan; *h, h, h*, the Pillars, as in the Plan C, *d, d, d*; E, g, the Plan of the Top of the Table; *f, f*, the Plan of the Mouldings *f, f*, which go round the Pillars: The Dimensions are specified.

PLATE LXXVII.

A Library-Table, with its Plan and Profile. The Drawers in the upper Part must draw out at each End of the Table. It has Doors on both Sides, with upright Partitions for Books, and Drawers on the other Side within the Doors. The hollow Corners must be fixed to the Doors; and to open with them. The Mouldings are at large, with a Scale.

PLATES LXXVIII. LXXIX.

Two Library-Tables, as above, with the Dimensions to them.

PLATE LXXX.

A Library-Table. The Ends form an Oval, with carved Terms fixed to the Doors, which must be cut at the Aftragal, and base Mouldings, to open with the Doors. On the Left are the Plan and the Upright, with some Variations in the Terms, and a Scale, with the Mouldings at large.

PLATES LXXXI. LXXXII.

Two Library-Tables. Plate LXXXII. hath a Writing-Drawer, which draws out at one End, and hath Term-Feet to fupport it, as may be feen at B, and are fixed at the End as in Plan A; C is a Top, which rifes with a double Horfe, to ftand to read or write upon; *e, e*, are the Horfe, with the Hinges marked: The Scale and Mouldings are at large.

PLATE LXXXIII.

A Library-Table, with circular Doors at each Corner. The other Doors and Terms, or Pilafters, are different, for the Sake of Variety. The Dimensions are specified, and Mouldings are at large.

PLATE LXXXIV.

Three Library-Tables. A hath three Drawers at Top on each Side, and Doors below; B hath three Drawers at Top on each Side, with a carved Feftoon of Flowers on the four end Drawers. The middle Drawer goes from Front to Front, for holding Maps, Prints, &c. The Doors may have carved Palm-Branches put on them. C hath its Ends in a curve Shape, and are made feparate, and fixed to the Top; the middle Drawer is fixed in afterwards: The Ornaments are

3

intended

intended for Brafs-Work. The Breadth is three Feet, or three Feet, two Inches. D is the Moulding for A, or C. The Moulding for B is on the right Hand, with a Scale.

PLATE LXXXV.

A Gothick Library-Table. The Corners are canted with proper Breaks, and three-quarter Pillars fixed on the Edges of the Doors, and they open with them.

PLATE LXXXVI.

Is the Plan of the above Table, with its Mouldings; *a, a, a,* are the Places where the Pillars are fixed. A is the Plan of the Pillars, and a Scale.

Figure 1 is a Method for working and mitering Mouldings of different Projection. Suppose B a Quarter of a Circle, or Moulding, divided into nine Parts, and the laft Divifion into two; then plan the Moulding B at D, and divide it into the fame Number of Parts, and draw the Diagonal, fuppofe L, L; and where the Divifions interfect in L, L, draw the Divifion in A; then raife Perpendiculars from A, and you have the Projection of the other Moulding at B. Now where the Perpendiculars, 1, 2, 3, 4, &c. interfect in B, draw *e, e, e,* to *d, d, d*; then where they interfect in *d, d, d*, are the Parts where the Moulding is to be traced, or drawn by Hand.

To cut the Mitres. Suppofe the Mouldings worked at F, F, and fit for the Mitres to be cut, draw a Line acrofs the Mouldings *f, f, f,* &c. then take the Diftance *c*, L, and fet it off at C, *f,* after the Divifions at A: then take the Diftance *e*, L, and fet it off at E, *f,* after the Divifions at D. Raife Perpendiculars at C and E; then draw the Parallels at *e, e, e,* to the Perpendiculars at C and E, and where they interfect, are the Points where you are to cut, directed by the Diagonal Line L, L.

PLATE LXXXVII.

Two Bookcafes. The little one is drawn in Perfpective. F, F, are two circular Doors, which make a Recefs for the Knees. B is a Drawer, which may have Conveniences for writing or dreffing at; the upper Door is intended to have a Glafs. A is a different Cornice for the Bookcafe, E, with a Scale to take off the Dimenfions. D is the Profile of it. The upper Doors are intended for Glafs.

PLATE LXXXVIII.

Is two Defigns of Bookcafes, with Glafs Doors in the upper Parts. They are drawn to an Inch Scale, and if it fhould be required to make them larger or lefs, it is only making a Scale more or lefs than an Inch, or to divide the whole Length into as many Feet, or Feet and Inches, as you require your Length to be: The fame Rule may be obferved in all the other Bookcafes. Thefe Cafes are fourteen or fifteen Inches deep, and the lower Part muft project four or five Inches more than the upper Part; at leaft they look better fo.

PLATE LXXXIX.

A Gothick Bookcafe. The upper Doors are intended for Glafs. A is the Plan of the Stile of the Door; D is the Gothick Pillars, glued to the Door; B the Plan of the upper Part; C the Plan of the under Part. The Mouldings are at large on the Left, with a Scale. E is a different Top for the middle Part. There muft be quarter Pillars in the internal Angles of the upper Part, and half Pillars at the back Corners, &c.

PLATES XC. XCI.

Two Bookcafes, with their Dimenfions and Mouldings at large in Plate XC. The Mouldings in Plate XCVI. are proper for XCI. If you are inclined to alter thefe Dimenfions, obferve the Rule given at LXXXVIII. and fo of all the others.

PLATE XCII.

A Bookcafe without Doors to the upper Part. The Truffes Pilafters, and Drops of Flowers are pretty Ornaments, as well as thofe on the Pediment, and of the bottom Doors: But all of them may be omitted, if required. The Scale and Profile are annexed.

PLATES

PLATES XCIII. XCIV.

Plate XCIV. contains the Mouldings at large for XCIII. and hath a Scale for getting the Mouldings for any of the Bookcafes. viz. Take the whole Height of the upper Part of the Bookcafe, and divide it into twenty equal Parts; one of which divide again into three equal Parts one Way, and into four the other (but any Breadth is the fame); then divide one of thofe three Parts into twelve equal Parts, as you fee fpecified: then draw a Diagonal from Corner to Corner, and in one of the Divifions to take off Quarters, Halves, and three Quarters. The Mouldings are drawn from this Scale.

PLATES XCV. XCVI.

Plate XCV. is a Bookcafe, with the Dimenfions: And Plate XCVI. contains the Mouldings at large, and a Scale, as mentioned in XCIV. There are different Mouldings for the Plinth and Surbafe on the left Hand.

PLATE XCVII.

A Gothick Bookcafe, with the Mouldings at large, and proper Centers to draw them by. A is the Plan of the Mouldings, which form the inner Work of the Doors, Half of which muft be wrought on the Stile of the Door.

PLATES XCVIII. XCIX.

A Bookcafe, with the Profile and Scale. Plate XCIX. is the Mouldings at large.

PLATE C.

A Gothick Bookcafe, with a Scale and Profile. The Mouldings and Capital are drawn Half their Bignefs, on the left Hand. The middle Pillars muft be glued, Part on one Door, and Part on the other, fo as the Doors may open. If the middle Pillar on the Right hath one of the three Rounds glued on the middle Door, the other two muft have their Bafes and Capitals cut or fcribed away behind, to let the glued one turn behind, and hung with Pin-Hinges at Top and Bottom. The Door on the Left muft have one of the Rounds of the Pillar glued upon it at the opening Side. If the Rounds, which compofe the Pillars that are glued on a fmall Round be left a little afunder, the Doors will open better, as you'll fee by the Plan. A is the Plan of the Pillar, B the Stile of the Door.

PLATES CI. CII.

A Gothick Bookcafe, with Gothick Pillars fixed on the Doors. The Capitals and Bafes remain fixed, fo that there can be no Difficulty in opening the Doors. Plate CII hath all the Mouldings at large, with a Plan of the Pillars on the Stiles of the Doors, and a Scale, as at Plate XCIV.

PLATE CIII.

Two Defigns of Organs for a Chamber. Organs of this Sort differ in Bignefs, according to the Rooms they are intended for, and the Number of Stops required in them.

PLATE CIV.

Two Organs; one Gothick, the other according to modern Architecture. They are very plain, and eafily comprehended.

PLATE CV.

An Organ fit for a fmall Church. The middle Part projects; the Breaks of the Pedeftals are in a circular Form to the End-Parts. The End-Parts go off at the out Corners, and make an Angle in Front, which may be perceived by the fhaded Parts of the Pedeftal. If the Ornaments on the Tower in the Center fhould be difapproved, they may be omitted. A Scale is annexed for the Particulars.

PLATE

PLATE CVI.

An Organ in the Gothick Tafte. As moft of the Cathedral Churches are of Gothick Architecture, it is Pity that the Organs are not better adapted. The Plan of the Pipes is below, and a Scale to take off the Dimenfions. The Pipes are returned upon the Out-Corners, as you may fee in the Plan, to complete the Spires; and if the Ends fall with the fame Sweep as in Front, it would have a good Effect.

PLATE CVII.

A Defk and Bookcafe in Perfpective. The under Part hath Doors and fliding Shelves within, for Cloaths: The upper Doors are intended for Glafs. A is the Infide of the Defk; C is the Profile of the Defk; B the Cornice, with a Scale.

PLATE CVIII.

A Defk and Bookcafe. The Door in the Middle of the upper Part is intended for Glafs: The middle Part of the Defk confifts of Drawers and Doors at the Ends, and within the Doors may be upright Partitions for Books. Dimenfions are fixed.

PLATE CIX.

A Defk and Bookcafe in the Chinefe Tafte. The Doors of the Bookcafe are intended for Glafs, and the Frets at Bottom may be two Drawers: The Dimenfions are fixed to the Defign.

PLATE CX.

A Defk and Bookcafe. The upper Doors are intended for Glafs. There may be either Doors or Drawers in the Front of the under Part. Dimenfions are fixed.

PLATE CXI.

A Defk and Bookcafe on a Frame. The large Mouldings at the Bottom of the upper Part may be two Drawers: The Infide of the Defk is below. Dimenfions are fixed.

PLATE CXII.

A Defk and Bookcafe. The upper Doors are intended for Glafs: Within the Doors, in the under Part, may be upright Partitions for Books. The middle Part is a Recefs for the Knees, and may have Drawers for Papers, &c. A is the Defk-Part, with Drawers, Doors, and Pigeon-Holes. The Mouldings are at large, with a proper Scale.

PLATE CXIII.

A Cheft of Drawers, and a Cloaths-Prefs, with fliding Shelves: The Fret in the Middle may be two Drawers. A is the Plan, with a Scale: The Mouldings are at large on the Right.

PLATE CXIV.

A Dreffing-Table, with a Bookcafe on the Top. The Fret in the under Part is a Drawer, with Conveniences for Writing or Dreffing. The Ends of the upper Part are different. A is the Profile; B the Depth of the Recefs for the Knees. The Mouldings are at large, and a Scale.

PLATE CXV.

A Table and Bookcafe, as above, only the under Part may be Doors, or Drawers: The Mouldings are at large, and a Scale.

PLATE

PLATE CXVI.

A Writing-Table and Bookcafe for a Lady. The upper Doors are intended for Glafs. The middle Feet come out with the Drawer, which hath a Slider covered with green Cloth, or Spanifh Leather, for writing upon. A is the Plan of the upper Part; B of the under Part. The Mouldings are at large, and a Scale. The circular Parts at the Ends may be Drawers.

PLATE CXVII.

A Writing-Table and Bookcafe, as Plate CXVI. A is Half the Plan of the upper Part. B of the under Part. The Mouldings are at large, with a Scale.

PLATE CXVIII.

A Toilet, or Drefling-Table, for a Lady. The Drefling-Drawer under the Glafs fhould be divided in the fame Manner, or nearly, as at C, in Plate LII. The end Parts open with Doors. In the Recefs are two Drawers. On the Top is a large Looking-Glafs, which comes to the Front with joint Hinges, and over it a Compartment; and on each Side, End-Parts, with Doors that reprefent Drawers. The Ornaments fhould be gilt in burnifhed Gold; or the whole Work may be japanned, and the Drapery may be Silk Damafk, with Gold Fringes and Taffels.

PLATE CXIX.

A Toilet, as above. The Glafs, made to come forward with folding Hinges, is in a carved Frame, and ftands in a Compartment, that refts upon a Plinth, between which are fmall Drawers. The Drapery is fupported by Cupids, and the Petticoat goes behind the Feet of the Table, which looks better. The ornamental Parts may be gilt in burnifhed Gold, or japanned.

PLATES CXX. CXXI.

Two Cabinets. The Mouldings are at large, and Dimenfions fixed. Plate CXXI. hath different Feet.

PLATE CXXII.

Two Defigns of Cabinets; that on the Left hath folding Doors: The Ornament which is on them will conceal the Joining. Thefe Ornaments may be Brafs, or Silver, finely chafed and put on; or they may be cut in Filligree-Work, in Wood, Brafs, or Silver. B is Half the Plan.

That on the Right has one Door in the Middle, and Drawers on each Side. All the Ornaments which are on the middle Door, at Top, Bottom, and two Sides, muft be fixed faft, and to open with it: The Feet, as well as all the ornamental Parts, muft be caft in Brafs, or Silver, &c. A is Half the Plan.

PLATE CXXIII.

An India Cabinet, with Drawers in the Middle, and different Doors at the Ends. The Frame is pierced through, but may be folid, and the Fret glued on. The Dimenfions are fpecified, and the Mouldings at large, with a Scale.

PLATE CXXIV.

A Gothick Cabinet. The Gothick Work at Bottom is intended for a Drawer. The middle Part at B is open, and hath Shelves with Frets on the Edges. The Dimenfions are fixed, and a Scale.

PLATE CXXV.

A Cabinet with Term-Feet. The middle Part is a Door, with Gothick Pillars fixed on, and open with the Door, and hath a Glafs, which may be either filvered or tranfparent. The Ornaments are carved Wood. The under Drawer at D goes the whole Length, is pierced through, but

but

but may be folid, and relieved, or funk, with a fmall Moulding wrought round.   C, B, A, are the Mouldings.   A Scale is annexed.

P L A T E   CXXVI.

A Cloaths-Prefs, and a Cloaths-Cheft.   The Prefs hath fliding Shelves, which fhould be covered with green Baize, to cover the Cloaths.   The Sizes are fixed, but are often made larger.

P L A T E S   CXXVII.   CXXVIII.

Four Cloaths-Chefts upon Feet.   They may open in Front, and have fliding Shelves, as in Plate CXXVI.

P L A T E   CXXIX.

A Cloaths-Prefs in two Parts.   The upper Part as CXXVI.   The under Part is Drawers for Linen, &c.

P L A T E   CXXX.

A Cloaths-Prefs in the Shape of a Commode.   The upper Part hath different Doors.   The Ornaments may be omitted, if thought fuperfluous.

P L A T E   CXXXI.

A Cloaths-Prefs with different Doors.   The under Part is in Shape, with carved Ornaments for the Feet, which go up the Corners.   B is the upper Part; A the under Part.   The Mouldings are at large, with a Scale.

P L A T E   CXXXII.

A China-Cafe, with Glafs in the Front and Ends, to fhew the China.   The Feet are cut through, but may be folid, and the Frets glued on as on the Rails.   The Rail in Front is divided into three Drawers.   The Dimenfions are fixed, and Mouldings at large.

P L A T E   CXXXIII.

A China-Cafe, as above.   The Canopy projects more at the Ends than Front.   For the Method of working, fee Fig. 1. Plate LXXXVI.   The Mouldings are at large, and a Plan of the Stile of the two Doors lapped together, as you will fee by the dotted Line.

P L A T E   CXXXIV.

A China-Cafe, as above.   The Profile is on the Right: Between the middle Feet is a fmall Canopy, for a Chinefe Figure, or any other Ornament.

P L A T E   CXXXV.

A large China-Cafe, with Glafs in the Doors and Ends.   The top Part is intended to be open in Front.   The Profile is on the Right, and a Scale.   The Ornaments on the Feet may be left out, and a Plinth put in their Stead.   This Piece of Work may be made of a foft Wood, and japanned, or painted and partly gilt.

P L A T E   CXXXVI.

A China-Cafe.   The Mouldings are on the Left, and the Dimenfions fixed.

P L A T E

PLATE CXXXVII.

A China-Cafe, very proper for a Lady's Dreffing-Room. It may be made of any foft Wood, and japanned any Colour. The middle Part hath two Doors, and the middle Stiles are lapped together, as in Plate CXXXIII.

It will be beft to make the Middle and Ends feparately, as alfo the upper Work of the Canopies, Frets, &c. The Feet are cut through; but the Rail of the Frame muft not, as it will be too weak to fupport fo large a Piece of Work. The Front and Ends are intended for Glafs. The Ends of the Canopies in the Middle project much more than in the Fronts: And for the Method of working and mitring, fee Plate LXXXVI. Fig. 2. The Mouldings are at large, and Dimenfions fpecified.

PLATE CXXXVIII.

Two Shelves, for Books or China. That on the Right is intended for Glafs in the Doors and Ends, as at C. B hath no Doors, nor Frets on the Edges of the Shelves, but may if defired: Under the End-Parts are carved Brackets, which make a good Finifhing. C is the Profile, with a Scale.

PLATE CXXXIX.

Two Shelves, as above. That on the Left hath a Fret-Door, with Glafs in it. The Fret at Bottom may be two Drawers. *b* is the Profile of B. That on the Right hath no Glafs in the Doors. *a* is the Profile of A. The Scale is annexed.

PLATE CXL.

Two Shelves, with Canopies, with their Plans and Scales.

PLATE CXLI.

A Shelf for China. The Canopy is a Kind of Dome, pierced through. The Plan, Profile, and a Scale are on the Right.

PLATE CXLII.

This Shelf is intended for japanning. The Fretwork at the Ends is defigned for Doors. The Supporters of the Canopies of the Ends ftand at the Corners, and are joined in the Middle. The Feet are pierced through. A is the Plan, with a Scale

PLATE CXLIII.

A Shelf, as above. The Plan and Scale are on the Left. The three Squares marked in the Plan, are the Sizes of the upper Shelves.

PLATE CXLIV.

Six Candleftands. They are from three Feet, fix Inches, to four Feet, fix Inches in Height. They have three Arms, and three Feet each, and the Sides are mitred together.

PLATE CXLV.

Four Candleftands, as above, which, if finely executed, and gilt with burnifhed Gold, will have a very good Effect.

PLATE CXLVI.

Four Candleftands. That in the Middle is in the Chinefe Tafte, and will hold feven Candles.

PLATE

PLATE CXLVII.

Four Candleftands, which may be converted into Terms for Bufts. That on the Left is intended for a Glafs Globe, fixed at the Bottom in a Piece of Ornament: The Socket for the Candle may be fixed on a Piece of Wood, which may go down the Term and be fo contrived as to be raifed up by a fmall Line and Pully.

PLATE CXLVIII.

Four Terms for Bufts, with the Plan below each, and a Scale.

PLATE CXLIX.

Three Stands for China Jars, and may be either gilt or japanned.

PLATE CL.

Six Pedeftals. Two have Emblems of War, and one of Mufick and Poetry.

PLATE CLI.

Four Cifterns. The Ornaments fhould be Brafs. The Ciftern at Bottom fhould be made of Wood, or Marble, and cut out of the Solid. The others may be made in Parts, and joined with the Brafs Work.

PLATE CLII.

A, B, C, D, E, Five Lanthorns, for Halls, Paffages, or Staircafes. Two of them are fquare; the others have fix Sides, and are generally made of Brafs, caft from wooden Moulds: A Scale is annexed.

PLATE CLIII.

Three Lanthorns. That in the Middle is very large. That on the Left is in the Form of an Egg; and that on the Right hath the Corners hollowed in, as may be feen by the Plan.

PLATES CLIV. CLV.

Ten Chandeliers. That on the Left in Plate CLV. hath only four Sides; all the others have fix Sides. The two at the Bottom of Plate CLIV. are folid; but I think the open ones preferable. They are generally made of Glafs, and fometimes of Brafs: But if neatly done in Wood, and gilt in burnifhed Gold, would look better, and come much cheaper.

PLATE CLVI.

Three Fire-fcreens. A and B have each two Leaves, which fold together, and the Fret which goes round the Paper is cut through. The other Screen ftands on a Pillar, and flides up and down.

PLATE CLVII.

Three Fire-fcreens, which ftand on four Feet, and are commonly called Horfe-Fire-fcreens. That on the Left flides up. The Wood-Work of all of them fhould be gilt in burnifhed Gold.

PLATE CLVIII.

Three Fire-fcreens. That on the Right hath two Leaves, which fold. The others have Pillars, and flide up and down.

PLATE

PLATE CLIX.

Six Tea-Chefts. The Ornaments fhould be of Brafs, or Silver: The Plans are below, with a Scale.

PLATES CLX. CLXI.

Nine Brackets for Bufts. Their Dimenfions cannot be fixed.

PLATE CLXII.

Three Brackets for Marble Slabs. A may be the front Rail to any of them.

PLATE CLXIII.

Two Clock-Cafes, with their Plans.

PLATE CLXIV.

Three Clock-Cafes. *a* is the Plan of the Head and middle Part of that on the Left; B is the Plan of the Pedeftals; and C of the Moulding which goes round it.

The Head-Part of that in the Middle is fupported by two Ionick Columns and Pedeftals. A, A, are the Columns, which may be hollow, and the Weights of the Clock go down them. For the opening Parts, you may cut the Columns in the Middle; one Half remains fixed, the other opers as a Door. C is the hollow Part, where the Pendulum fwings. B, B, B, the Glaffes. A, A, at the Back are two Pilafters: on the Top are fome Emblems of Time. That on the Right, hath a Serpent, that goes round the Dial-Plate, reprefenting Time lafting to Eternity, and the Wings on the Sides fhew how fwiftly it flies away.

PLATE CLXV.

Two Table Clock-Cafes, with a Scale, and Half of their Plans. C is the Plan of that on the Left; B is the Plan of the Bafe; A is the Plan of the Cornice; *c, f,* the Plans of the Columns. The Ornaments which go round the Glafs on the Left, muft be a Door.

PLATE CLXVI.

Five Clock-Cafes. That in the Middle is very large, and fit for a Public Hall, or an Affembly-Room. The other are for Spring-Clocks.

PLATES CLXVII. CLXVIII. CLXIX.

Pierglafs-Frames, with a Scale, but the Dimenfions cannot be determined.

PLATE CLXX.

A Table and Pierglafs. A fkilful Carver may, in the Execution of this and the following Defigns, give full Scope to his Capacity.

PLATE CLXXI.

Two Frames of Pierglaffes.

PLATE CLXXII.

Four oval Frames.

PLATE CLXXIII.

Two Architrave Frames, with Heads.

PLATE

PLATE CLXXIV.

Two Ovals.

PLATE CLXXV.

Four Frames of Tables.

PLATE CLXXVI.

Two Frames of Tables. The uppermoft is a Dorick Entablature, with its Triglyphs and Metopes, fupported by two Cariatides. The undermoft is fupported by two piping Fauns, leaning againft two Vines, intermixed with Foliage, &c. It will have a grand Appearance, if executed with Judgment, and neatly gilt.

PLATE CLXXVII.

Five Girandoles.

PLATE CLXXVIII.

Three Girandoles. That on the Left is a Piece of Ruins intermixed, with various Ornaments.

PLATE CLXXIX.

Two carved Chimney-Pieces, with Glaffes, Frames, and other fuitable Ornaments.

PLATE CLXXX.

Two Chimney-Pieces in Architecture, with the Plans of the Columns below. The Columns may be whole.

PLATE CLXXXI.

Two Chimney-Pieces, with Glaffes.

PLATE CLXXXII.

A Chimney-Piece, which requires great Care in the Execution. The Imboffments muft be very bold, and the Foliage neatly laid down, and the whole properly relieved. The Top may be gilt, as likewife fome other ornamental Parts.

PLATE CLXXXIII.

A Chimney-Piece of Architecture, intermixed with Trophies, &c.

PLATE CLXXXIV.

A Chimney-Piece compofed of Architecture, Sculpture, and Ruins. Great Care will be neceffary in executing the upper Part: The Ornaments muft be carved very bold, fo that the Ruins may ferve as Bafs Relief. The under Part fhould likewife be very bold, and the Dog entirely free. It would not be amifs, if the whole was modelled before it is begun to be executed.

PLATE CLXXXV.

A Frame for a Picture. The Corners are Trophies of Hunting, Mufick, &c.

PLATE CLXXXVI.

A Frame with warlike Trophies in the Corners and Middles.

PLATE

PLATE CLXXXVII.

A Frame for a Picture of an Engagement at Sea.

PLATE CLXXXVIII.

Two Tabernacle-Frames proper for Stair-Cafes.

PLATE CLXXXIX.

Eight Shields, which, as they are often placed very high, fhould be very bold. They may ferve as Ornaments to Pediments.

PLATES CXC. CXCI.

Eight Stove-Grates. I would recommend the ornamental Parts to be of wrought Brafs, and as they may be made to take off, will be eafily cleaned.

PLATES CXCII. CXCIII.

Eight Defigns of Frets.

PLATES CXCIV. CXCV.

Ten Defigns of Borders for Paper-Hangings.

PLATE CXCVI.

Three Defigns of Fret-Work.

PLATES CXCVII. CXCVIII.

Four Defigns of Chinefe-Railing. They are genteel Fences for Gardens, &c.

PLATES CXCIX. CC.

Defigns of Handles and Scutcheons, of Brafs-Work, for Cabinet-Work. A and B are Handles for Tea-Chefts.

To His Royal Highness

PRINCE William Henry &c. &c. &c.

May it please your Royal Highness,

To take the Following Work under Your Protection.

Your Royal Highness's Ready Condescension to encourage
whatever is Laudable and useful, in every Art and profession, emboldens
the Author to lay it at Your Royal Highness's Feet, as it gives him,
an opportunity of assuring Your Royal Highness, that he is, with
the profoundest Respect

Your Royal Highness's

Most Obedient,

Most Devoted,

and

Most dutiful Servant

Thomas Chippendale

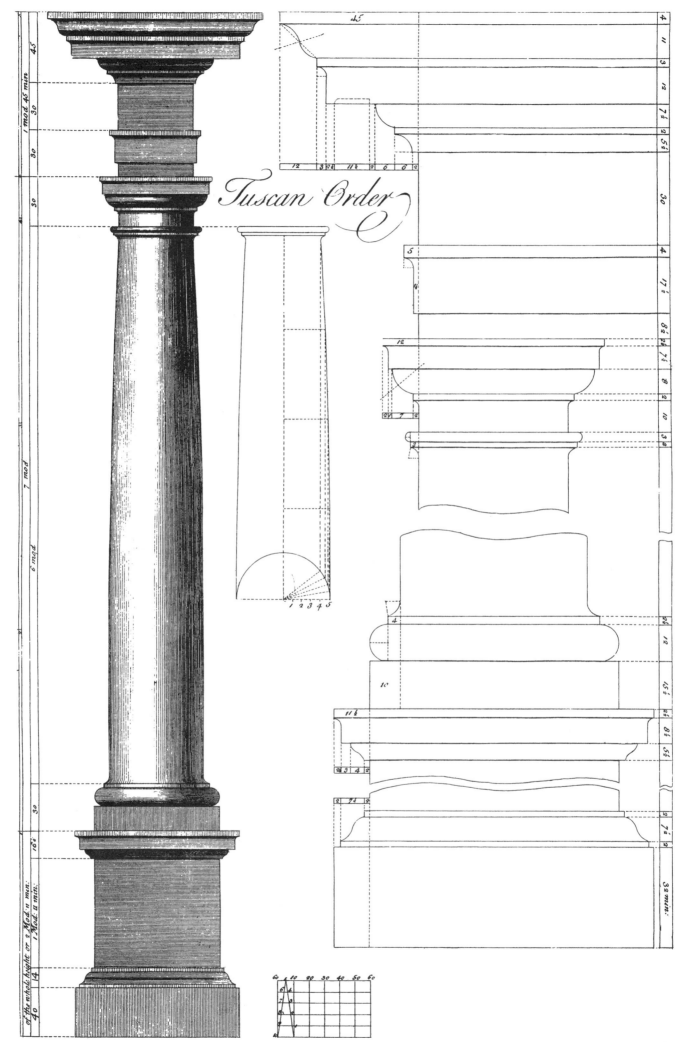

Tuscan Order

T. Chippendale inv. et del.   Pub. according to Act of Parliam. 1753   T. Müller sculp.

Doric Order

1 mod:

Ionic Order

T Chippendale inv et del

Pub: according to Act of Parliam. 1758

T Müller sculp

Corinthian Order.

IIII

T. Chippendale inv. et del.

Pub. according to Act of Parliam. 1753.

T. Müller sculp.

Composite
Order

T. Chippendale inv.t et del   Pub. according to Act of Parliam 1753.   T. Muller sculp.

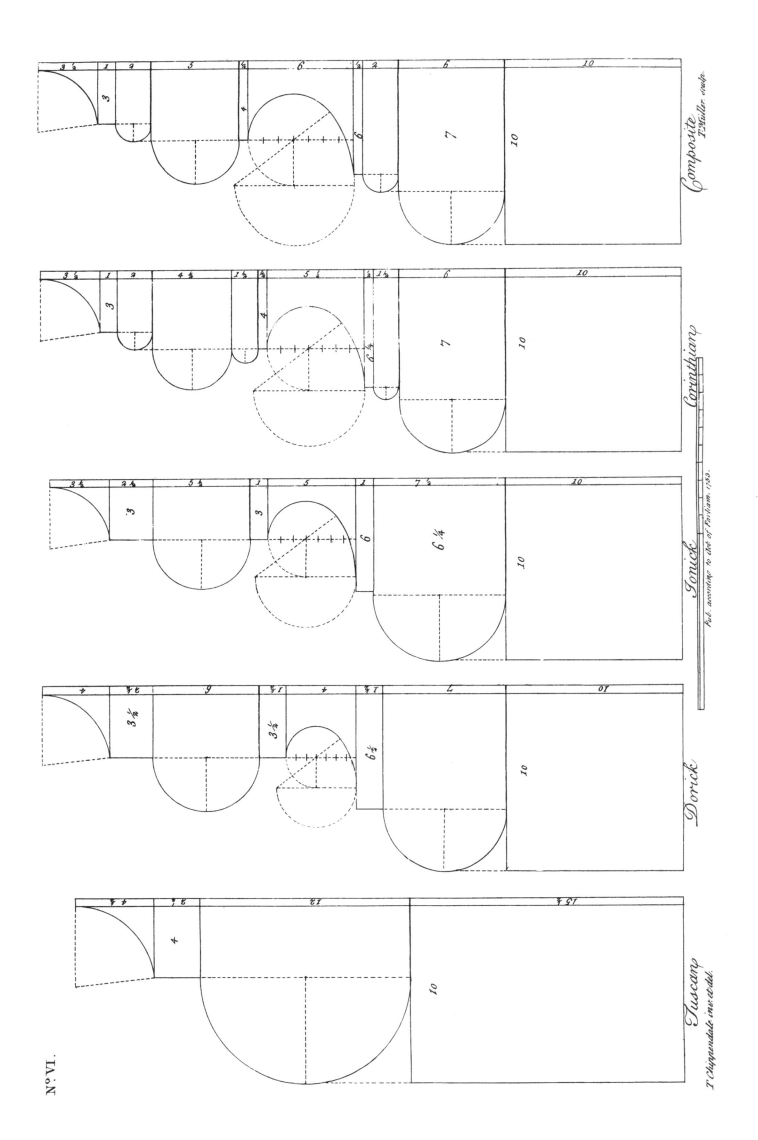

Composite T. Miller excudt.

Corinthian

Ionick

Pub. according to Act of Parliam. 1753.

Dorick

Tuscane
T. Chippendale invt. et del.

Nº VI.

Composite

Corinthian

Ionick

Dorick

Tuscan

T. Müller sculp.

Pubᵈ: according to Act of Parliament 1753.

T. Chippendale inv. et del.

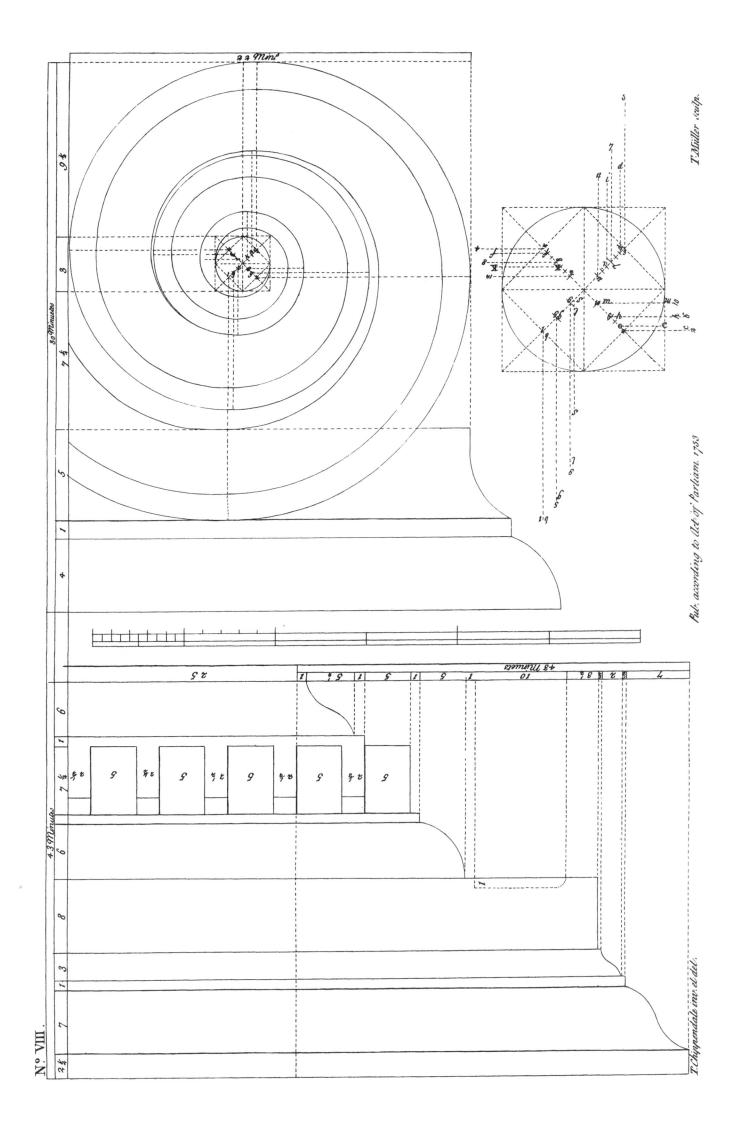

N.º VIII.

T. Chippendale inv. et del.

Pub. according to Act of Parliam. 1753.

T. Müller sculp.

Chairs.

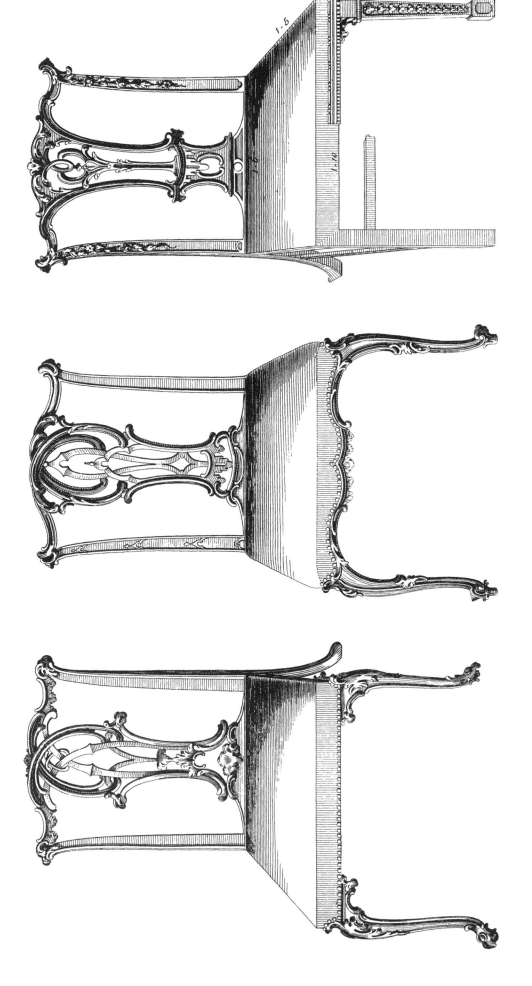

1.5

1.4

1.w

H. Chippendale. inv: et del.

Hemerich Sculp.

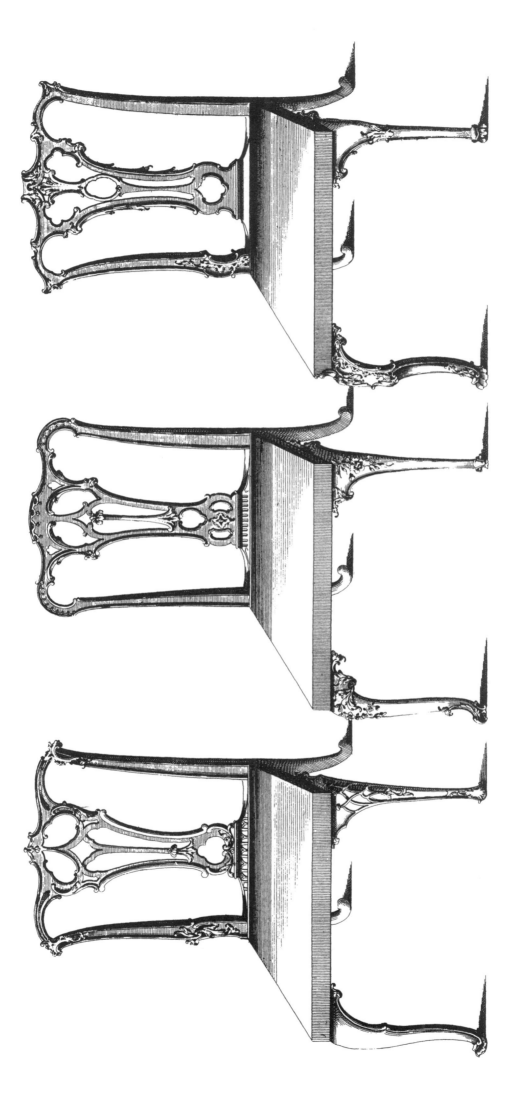

N.° X.

Chairs.

T. Chippendale inv.^r et delin.

publ.^d according to Act of Parliam.^t 1753.

W. Darly sculp.^t

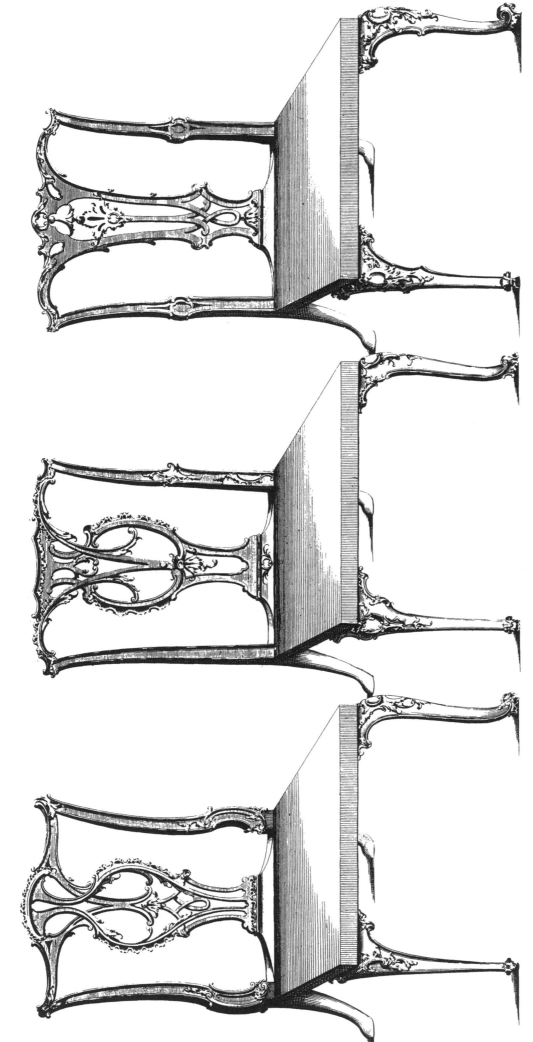

Chairs.

T. Chippendale Inv. t et del.

Pub.d according to Act of Parliament 1753

T. Darly sculp. t

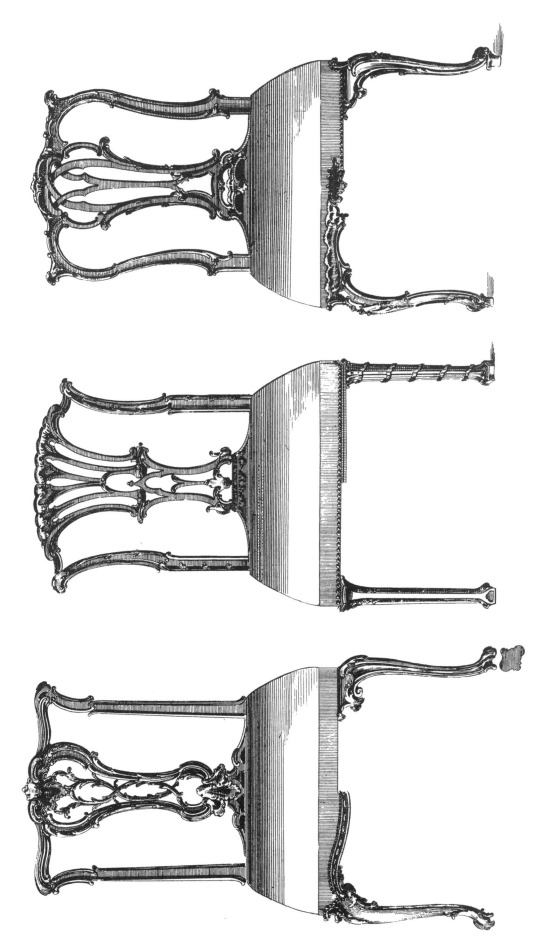

Chairs

Chippendale Inv. et Del.

Clews sculp.

Chairs.

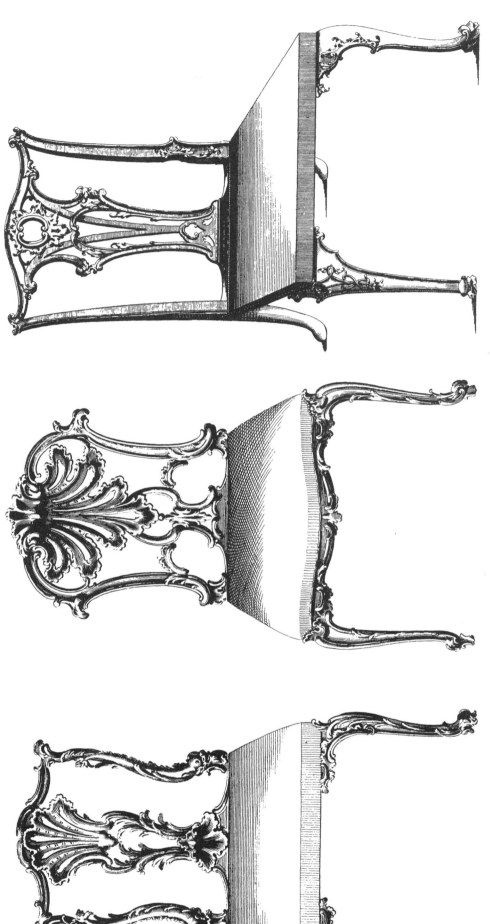

T. Chippendale inv'd del

Pub.d according to Act of Parliam.t 1761.

J. Taylor Sculp.

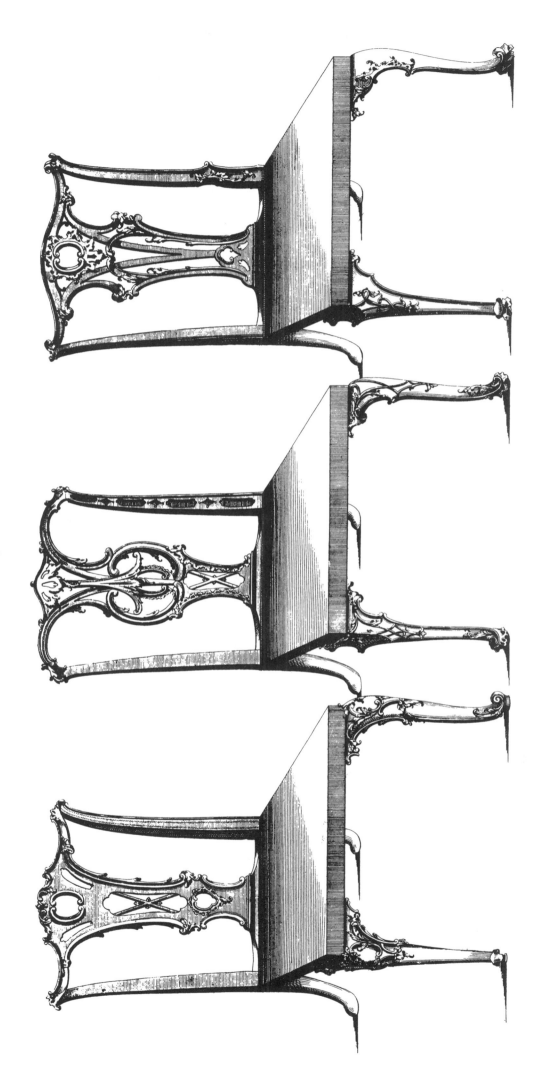

Chairs.

T. Chippendale inv.t et del.

Pub.d according to Act of Parliam.t 1753.

T. Darly sculp.

Hall Chairs.

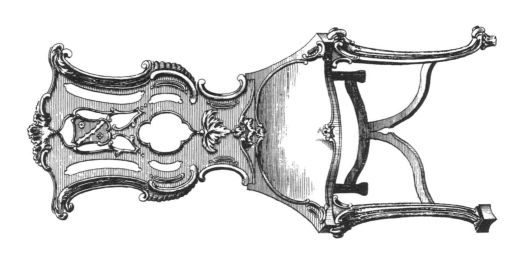

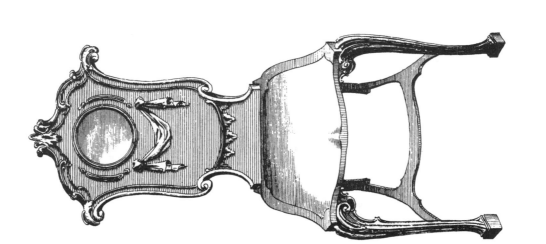

I. Miller sculp.

J. Chippendale inv.t et del.

Hall Chairs.

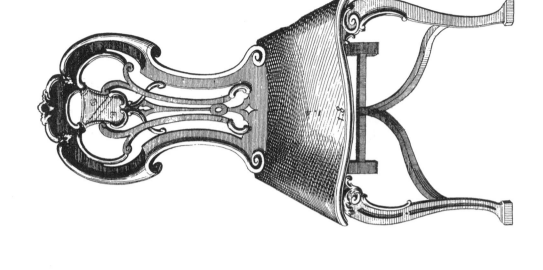

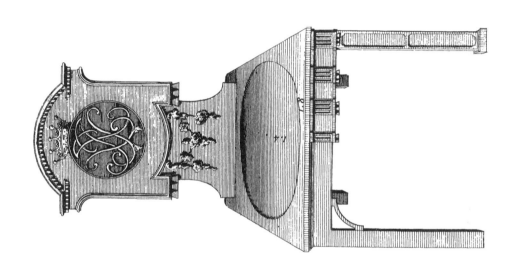

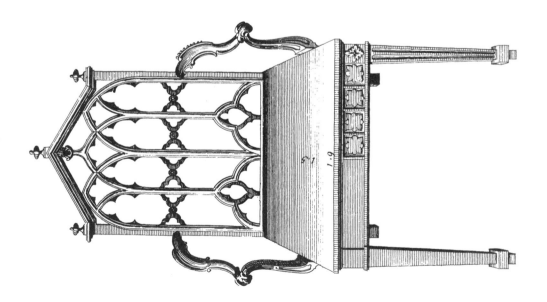

T. Chippendale inv.t et del.

Pub.d according to Act of Parliam.t 1759.

I. Taylor Sculp.

Backs of Chairs

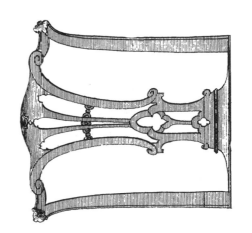

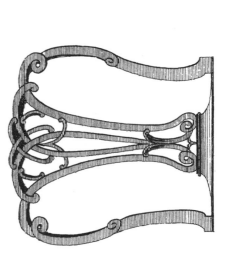

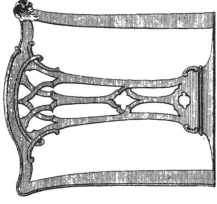

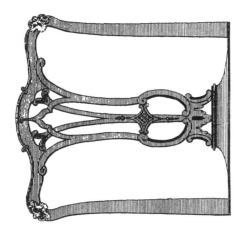

Miller Sculp.

T. Chippendale inv. et del.

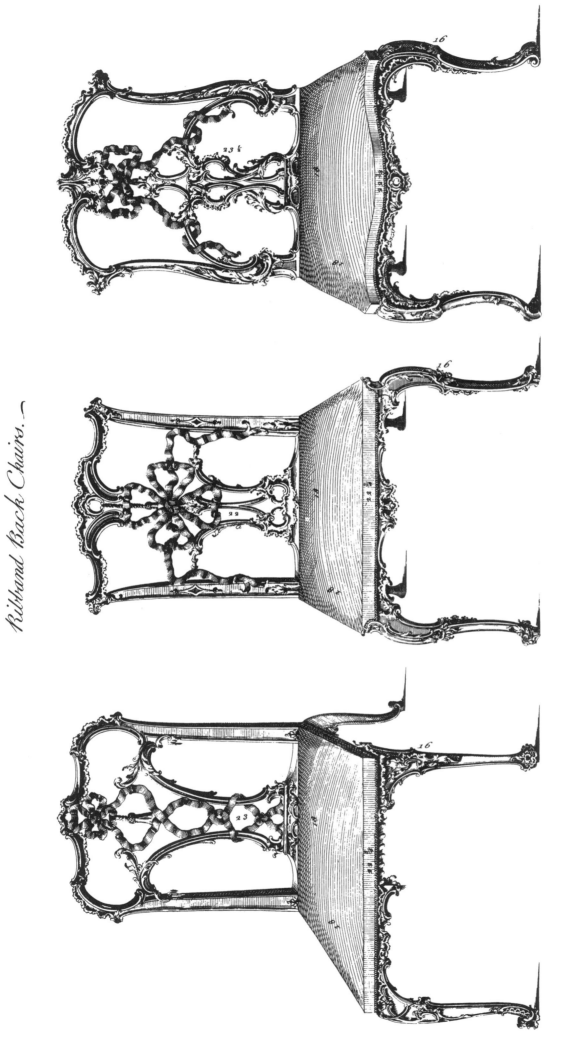

Ribband Back Chairs.

N.o XV.

T. Chippendale invt. et del.

Publish'd according to Act of Parliment

M. Darly Sculp.

French Chairs.

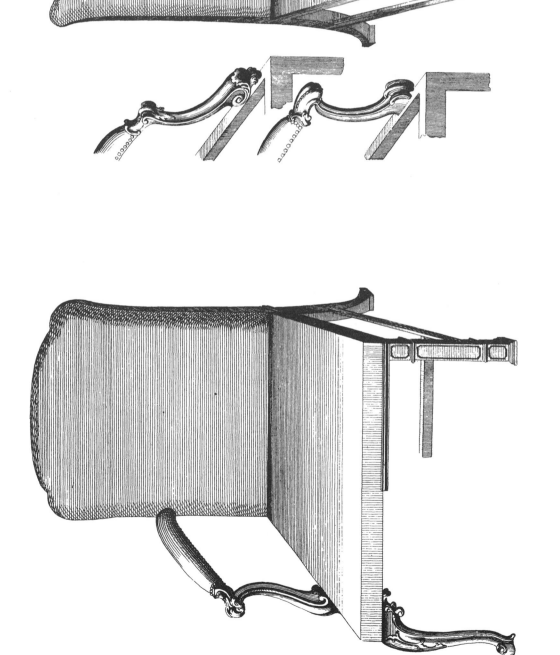

T. Chippendale inv.t et del.

I. Taylor sculp.

French Chairs

T: Chippendale invᵗ et delᵗ

Pubᵈ according to Act of Parliamᵗ 1753.

W Darly sculp

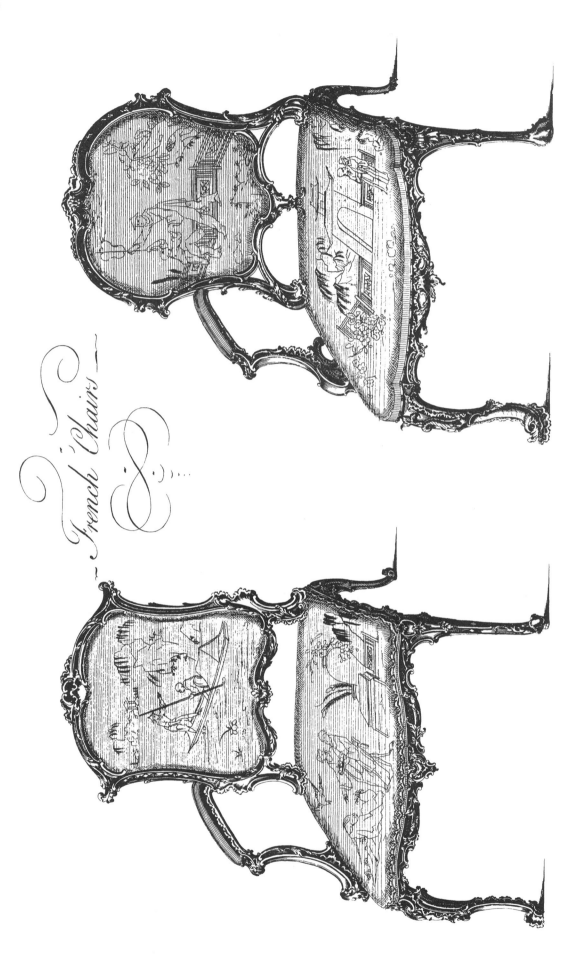

French Chairs

Chippendale inv.t et del.

Pub. according to Act of Parliam.t 1753

Darly sculp

French Chairs.

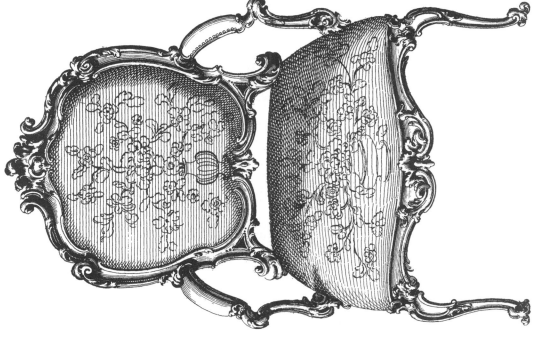

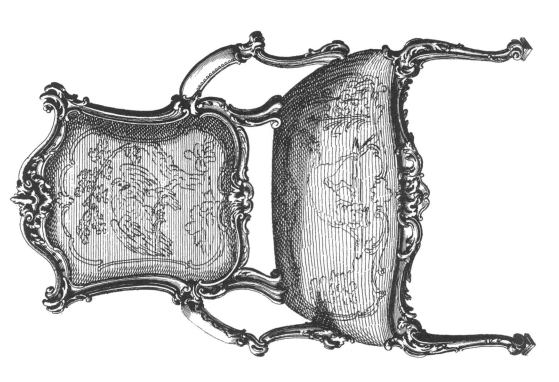

T. Taylor sculp.

T. Chippendale inv.t et delt.

Pub: according to Act of Parliam.t 1759.

French Chairs.

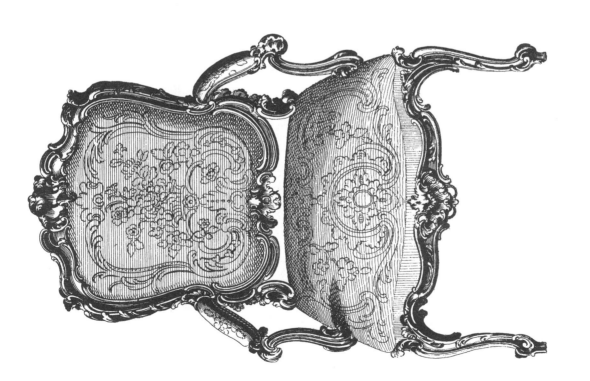

T.Chippendale inv.t et del.

Publish'd accord.t to Act of Parliament 1759.

T.Taylor sculp.

Designs for Garden Seats.

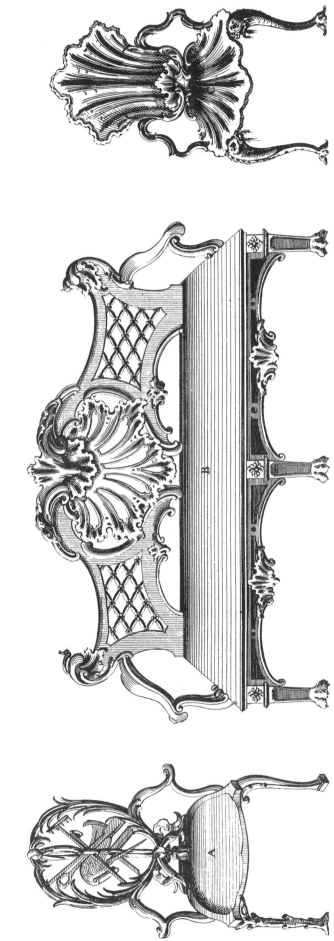

J.Chippendale inv.t et delin.

Publish'd according to Act of Parliment 1761

M.Darly Sculp.

Designs of Chairs.

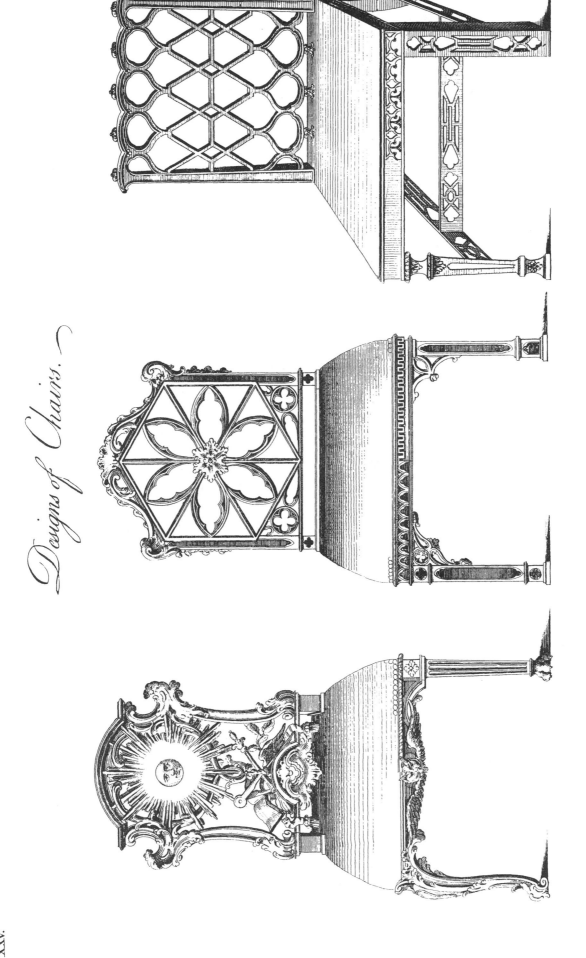

T. Chippendale inv. et delin.

Published according to Act of Parliament 1761.

M. Darly Sculp.

Chinese Chairs.

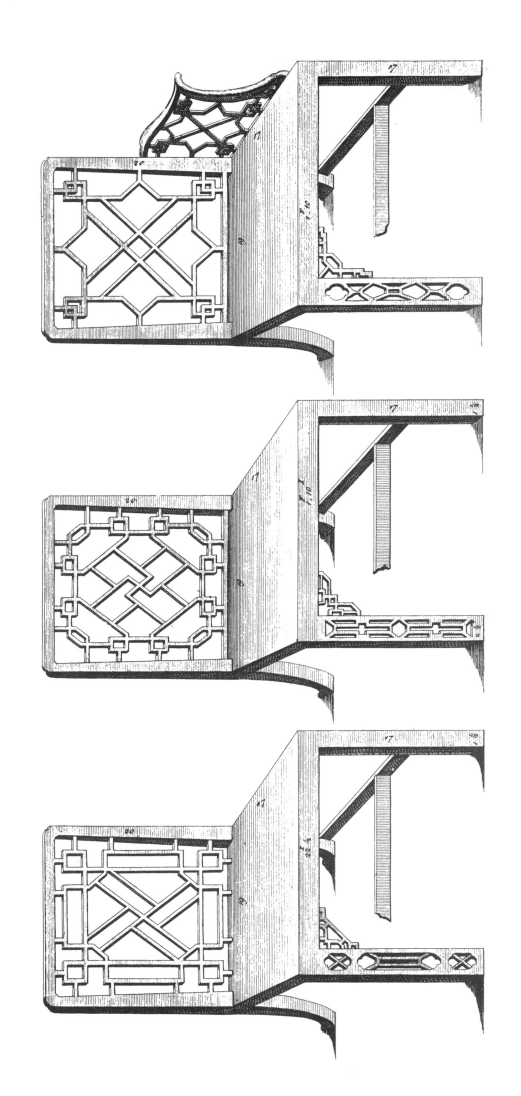

T. Chippendale inv: et delin.

Published According to Act of Parliament

M. Darly Sculp.

Chinese Chairs.

T. Chippendale inv. et del.

Publ.d according to Act of Parliam.t 1753

J. Darly sculp.t

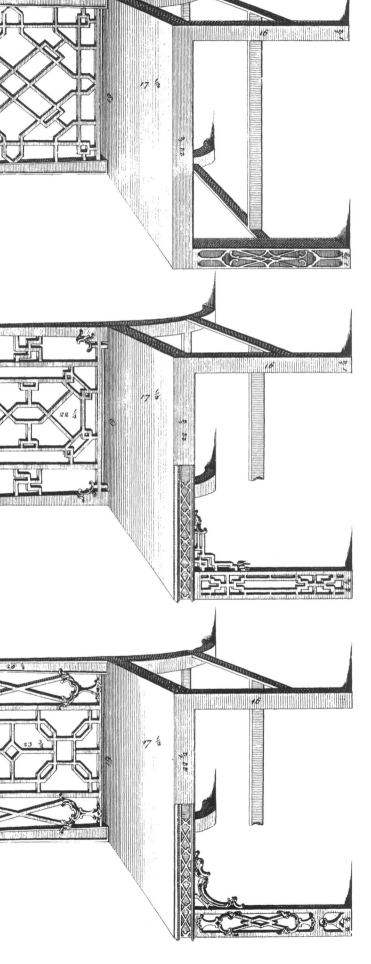

N.º XXVIII.

Chinese Chairs.

T. Chippendale inv. et delin.

Published According to Act of Parliament

M. Darly Sculp.

Sofas.

T. Chippendale inv.ᵗ et del.   Publish'd accord.ᵍ to Act of Parliament 1759.   J. Taylor sculp.

Sofas.

T. Chippendale inv.t et del.   Publish'd according to Act of Parliament 1759.   I. Taylor sculp.

A Sofa

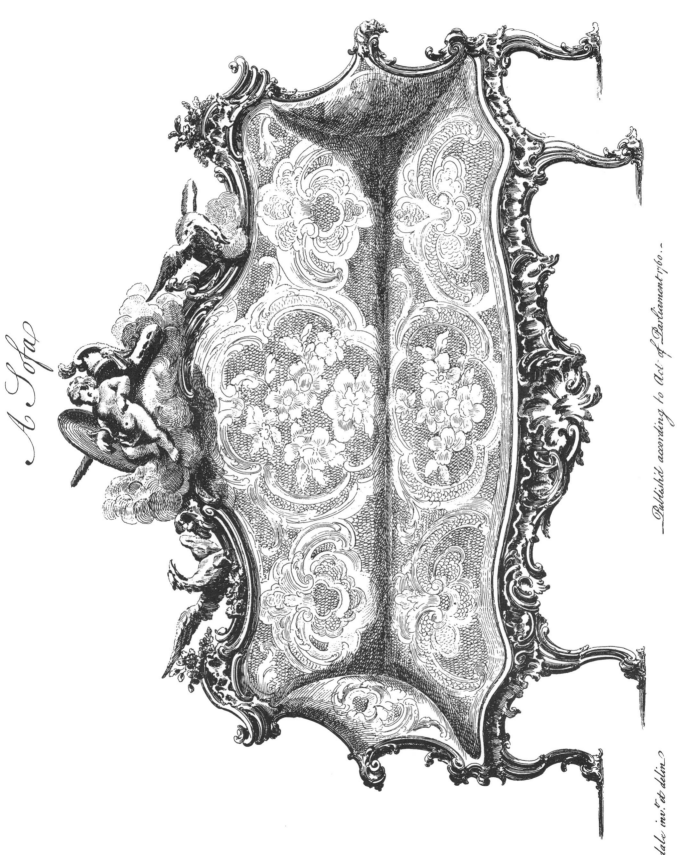

T Chippendale inv.t et delin

B: Clowes Sculp

Published according to Act of Parliament 1760.

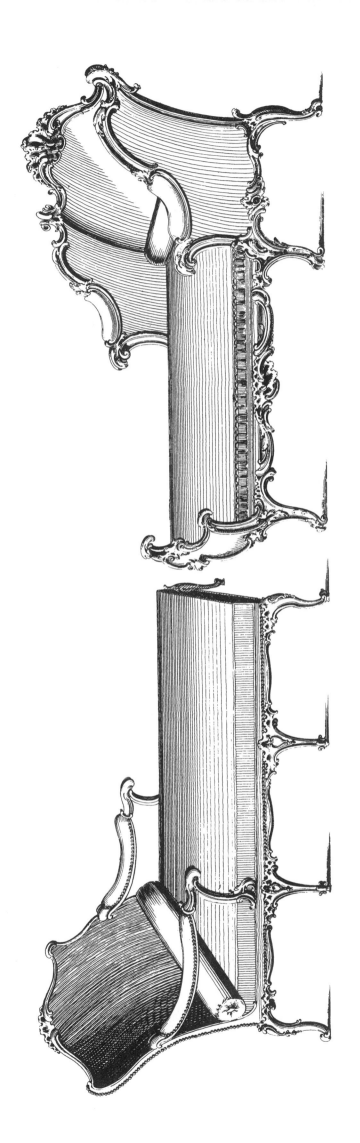

Designs for Couches.

J. Chippendale inv.t et delin

Darly Sculp.t

Publish'd according to Act of Parliam.t 761.

Chinese Sopha.

T. Chippendale inv. et del.

M. Darly Sculp.

Publish'd according to Act of Parliment

Bed Pillars

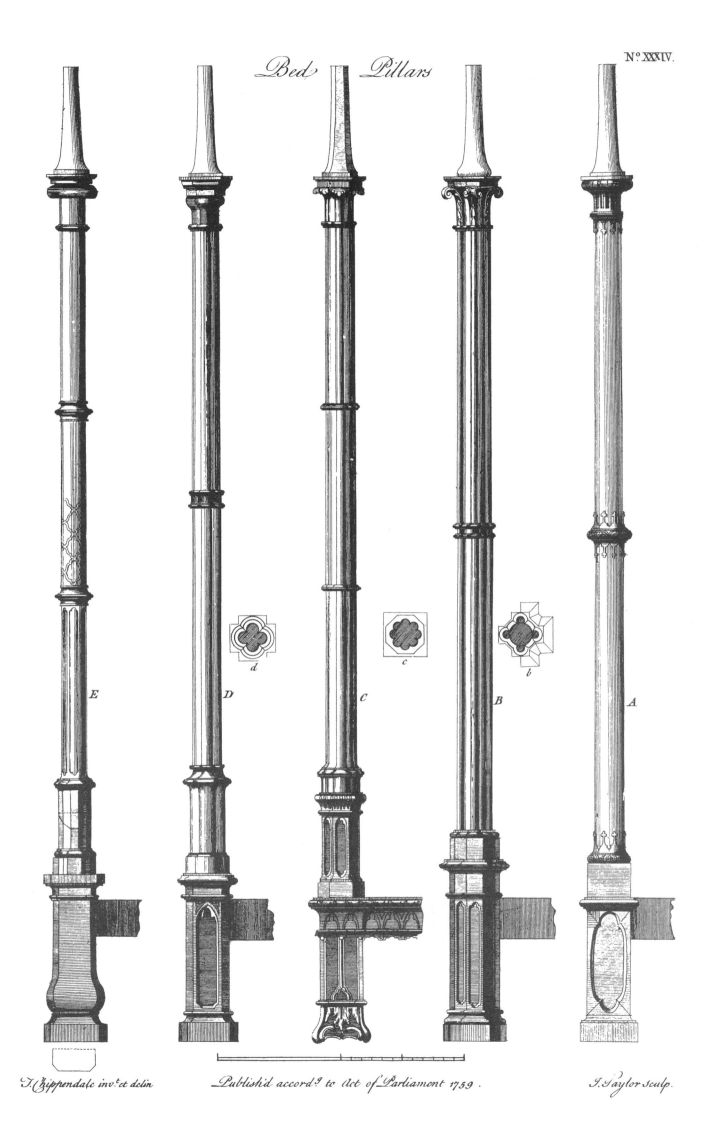

d   c   b

E   D   C   B   A

T. Chippendale inv.t et delin   Publish'd accord.g to Act of Parliament 1759.   T. Taylor sculp.

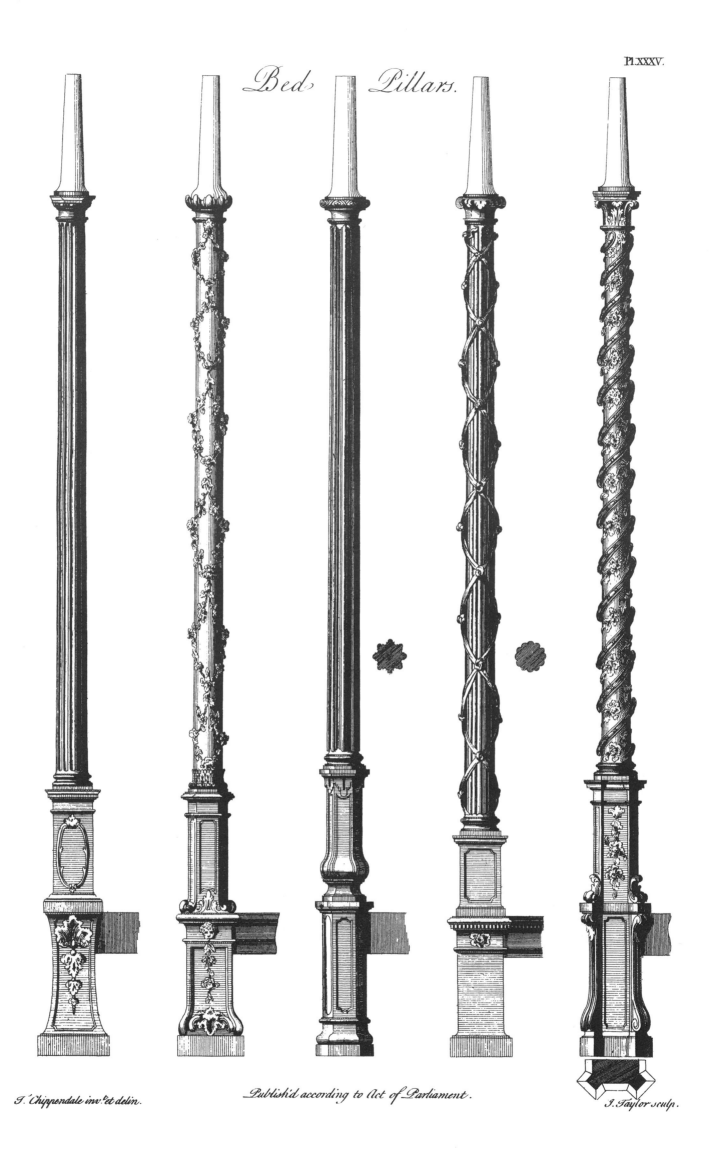

Bed Pillars.

Pl.XXXV.

J. Chippendale inv.t et delin.

Publish'd according to Act of Parliament.

J. Taylor sculp.

A Design for a Cornice for a Venetian Window

J. Chippendale invt. et del.

Publish'd According to the Act. 1762.

J. Taylor sculp.

Cornices for Beds or Windows.

J. Taylor sculp.

Publish'd according to Act of Parliament 1759.

T. Chippendale invᵗ et del.

A Bed.

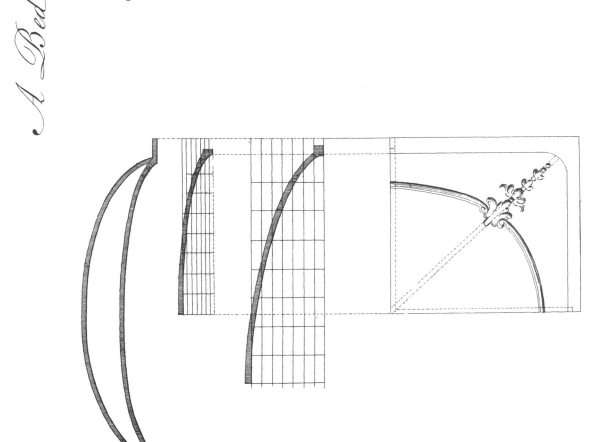

T. Chippendale inv.t et del.t

Publish'd according to Act of Parliament 1759.

J. Taylor Sculp.

A Bed.

T. Chippendale invᵗ. et del.   Publish'd accordᵍ to Act of Parliament 1759.   J. Miller sculp.

A Bed.

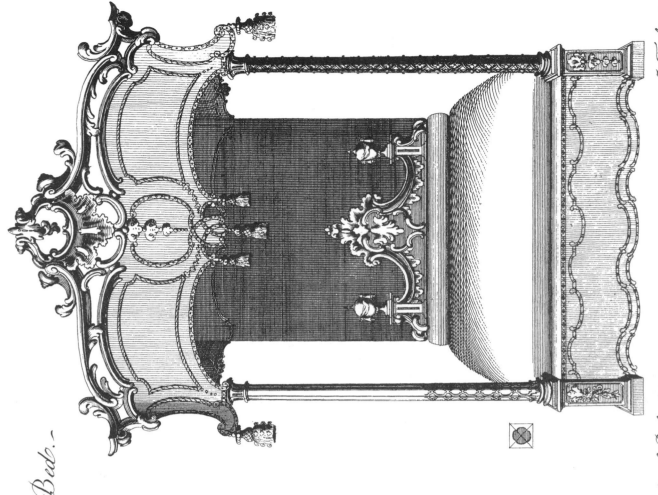

T. Chippendale inv.t et del.

Pub: according to Act of Parliam.t 1759.

I. Taylor Sculp.

No. XXI.

Bed.

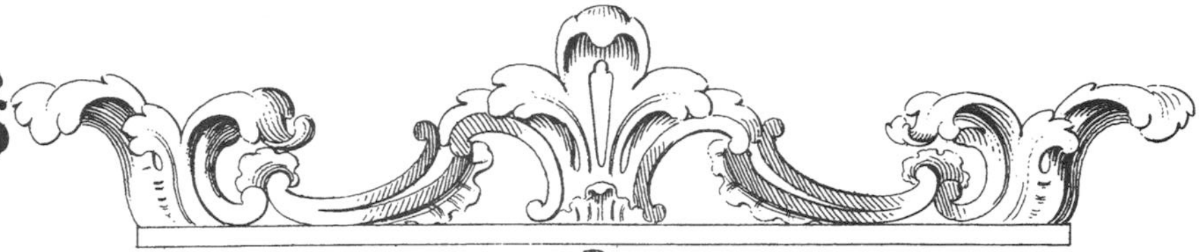

B

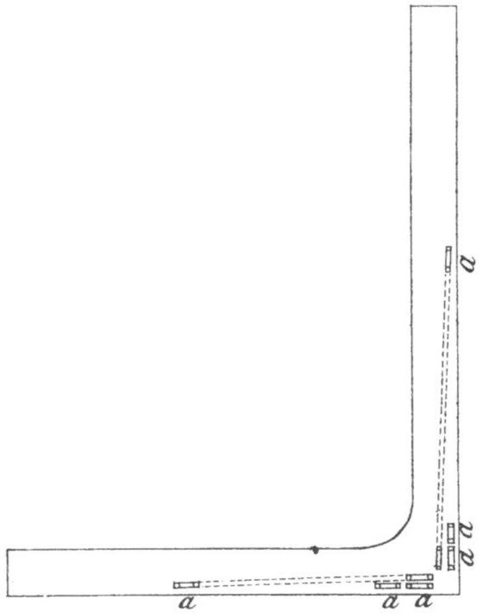

T. Chippendale inv.t et del.t.

Pub.d according to Act of Parliam.t 1753.

J. S. Müller Sculp.t

Canopy Bed

J.S. Müller Sculpit

T. Chippendale inv.t et del

Publ.d according to Act of Parliam.t 1753.

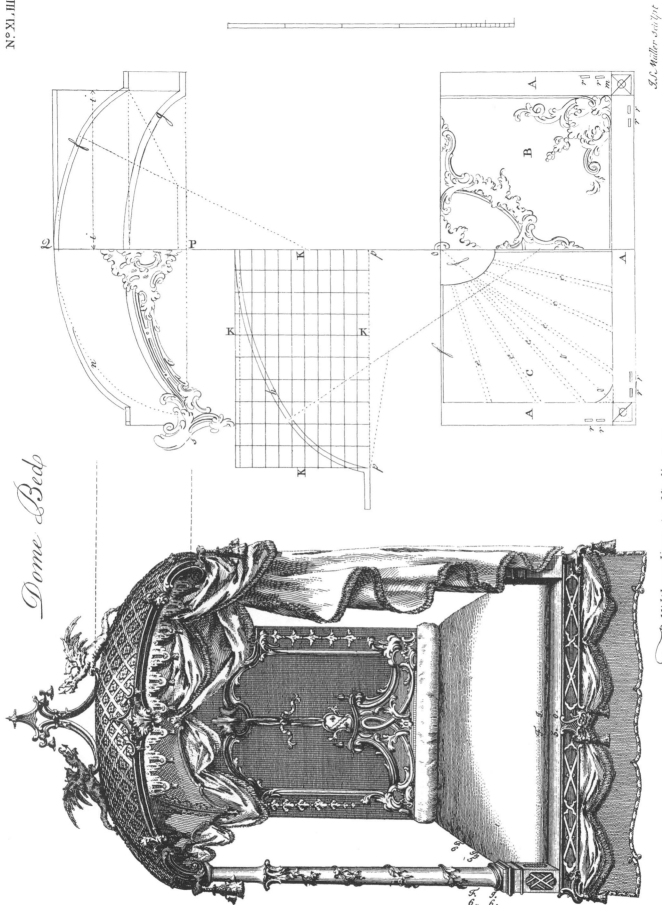

Dome Bed

J.C. Müller Sculpt.

Publish'd according to Act of Parliam.ᵗ 1753.

T. Chippendale invᵗ et del.

Gothick Bed.

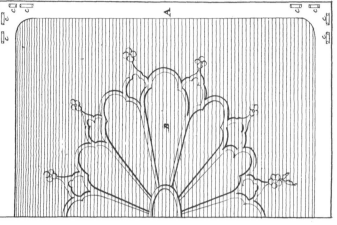
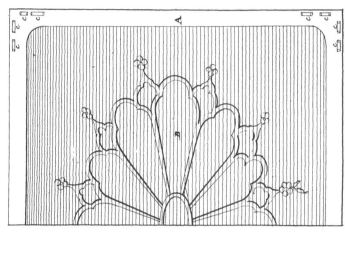

M. Darly Sculp.

Published according to Act of Parliament.

T. Chippendale invt et del.

T. Chippendale invᵗ et delin.   Publish'd according to Act of Parliament 1762.   Isaac Taylor Sculp.

No. XLVI.

A Couch Bed

E. Rocker Sculp.

Published according to Act of Parliament 1759.

T. Chippendale invt. et del.

A Design for a State Bed.

T. Chippendale invᵗ et delin. Published according to Act of Parliament, 1761. J. Taylor sculp.

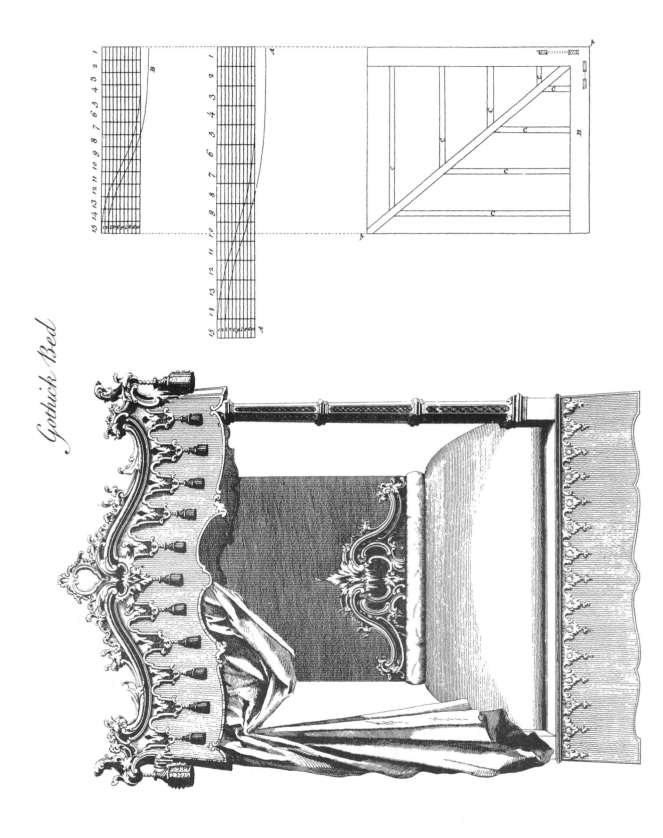

Nº XLVIII

Gothick Bed

T. Chippendale invt. et del.

Published according to Act of Parliament

I. S. Müller Sculp.

Designs for Field Beds.

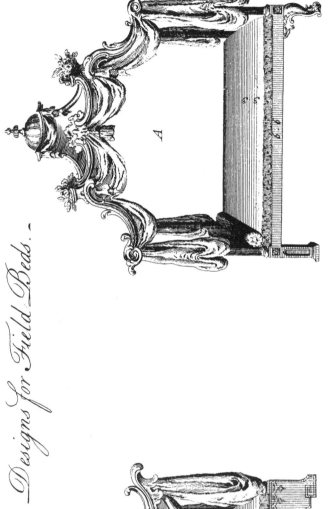

A

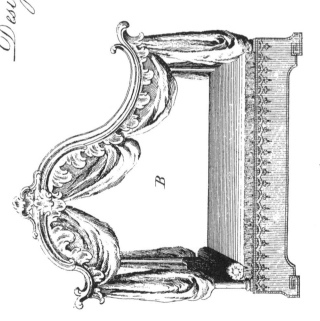

B

C

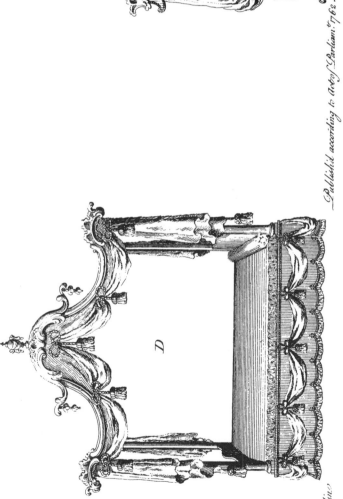

D

T. Chippendale inv. et delin.

Published according to Act of Parliam.t 1762.

Isaac Taylor Sculp.

A Couch Bed.

J. Chippendale inv.t et delin ___Publish'd according to Act of Parliam.t 1760.- ___Darly Sculp.

China Tables.

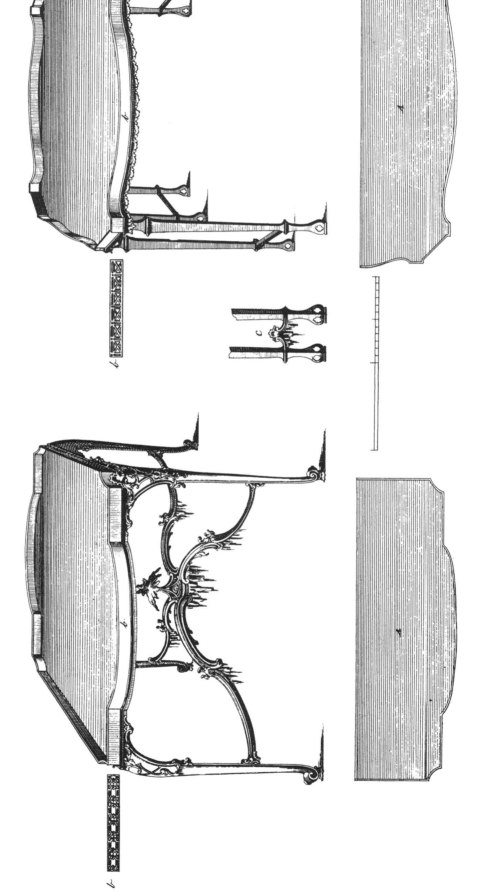

T Chippendale inv.t et del.t

Published according to Act of Parliament

M. Darly Sculp.t

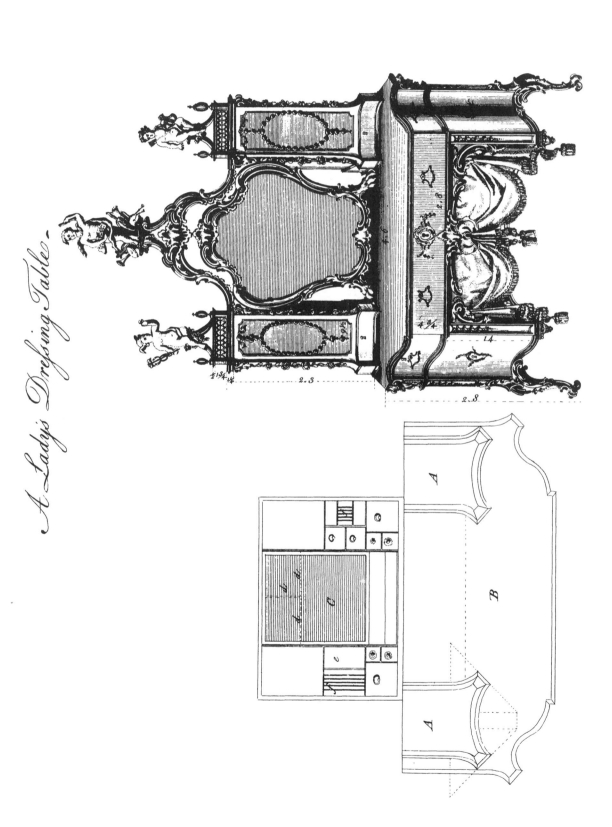

A Lady's Dressing Table.

T. Chippendale inv.t et delin.

Published according to Act of Parliament 61.

W. Foster Sculp.

Breakfast Tables.

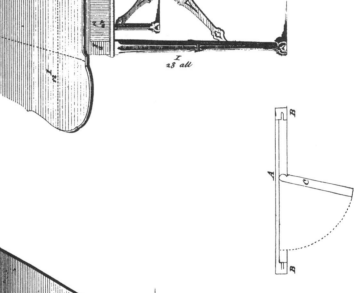

T. Chippendale invt. et delt.

Publish'd according to Act of Parliment

M. Darly Sculp.

A Shaving Table

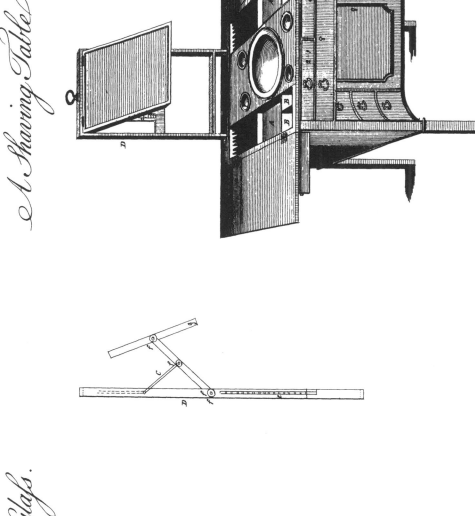

A Bason Stand & Glass.

Published according to e Act of Parliament 1761.

W. Foster sculp.

T. Chippendale inv. et delin.

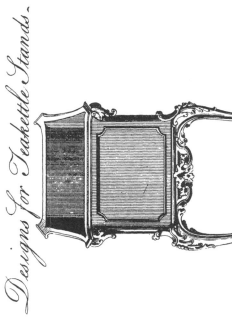

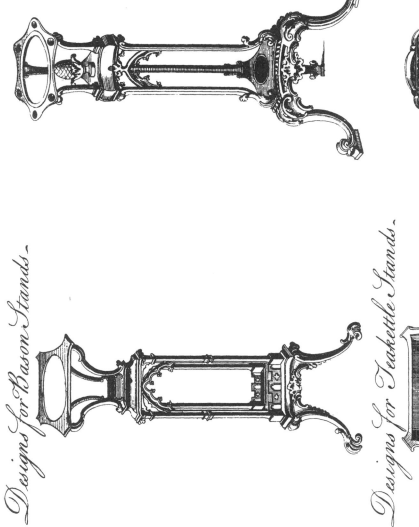

Designs for Bason Stands.

Designs for Teakettle Stands.

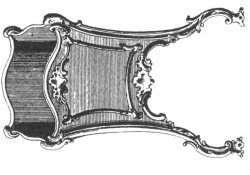

Darly Sculp.

Published according to Act of Parliament 1761.

T. Chippendale invt. et delin.

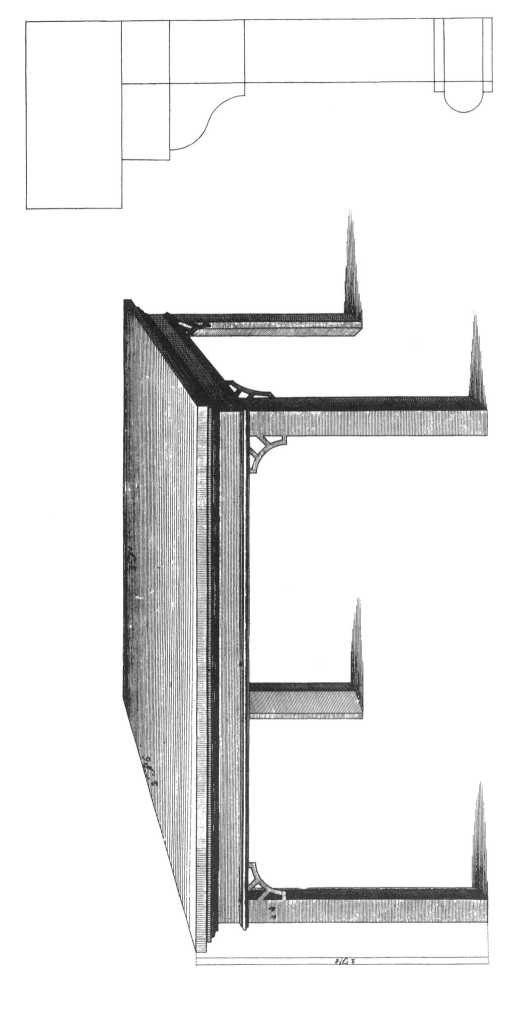

Sideboard Table.

Nº LVI.

T. Shippendale inv.t & del

Publ.d according to Act of Parliam.t 1.1.59

Sideboard Table.

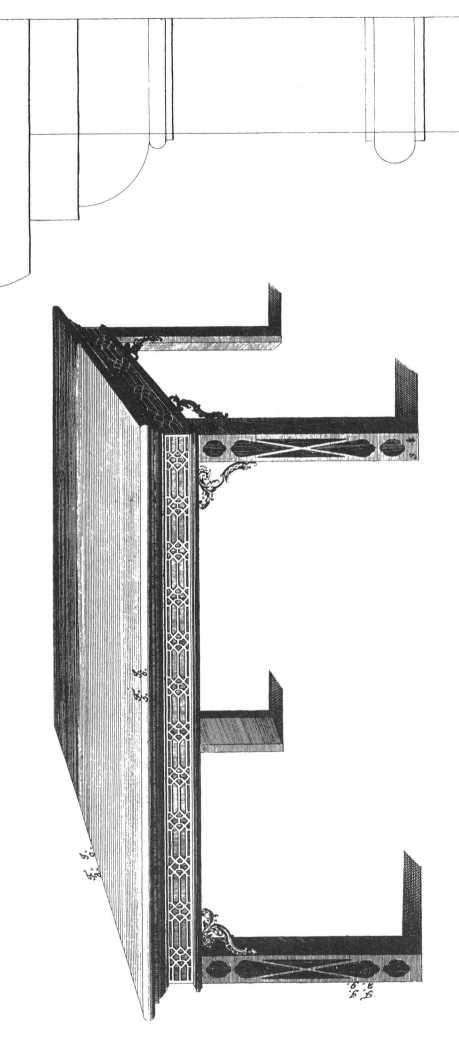

T. Chippendale inv. et del.

Publish'd according to Act of Parliament 1753.

M Darly sculp

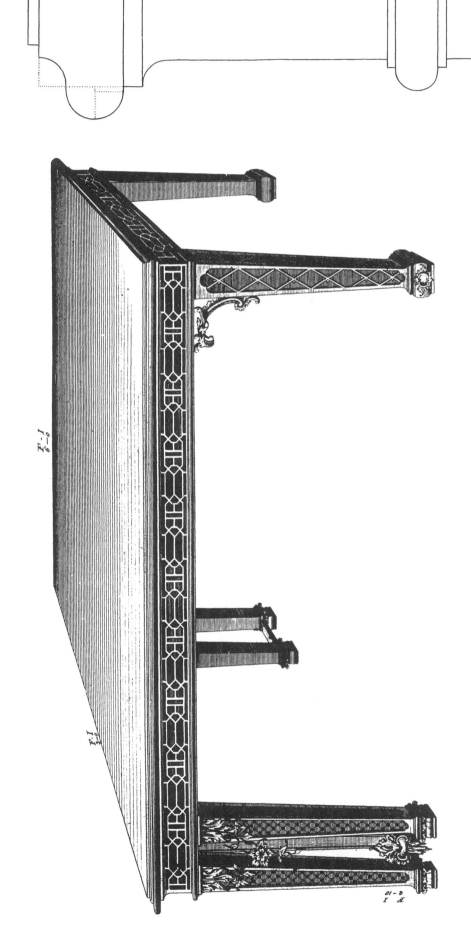

Side Board Table

I.S.Müller sculp.

Pub. according to Act of Parliament 1753.

T. Chippendale inv. et del.

Sideboard Table

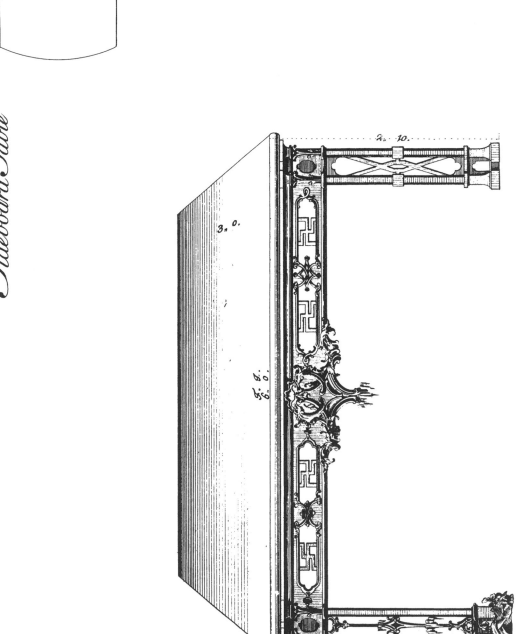

2, 10.

3, 0.

T. Chippendale inv.^t et del

Publ.^d according to Act of Parliam.^t 1753.

M.Darly sculpt

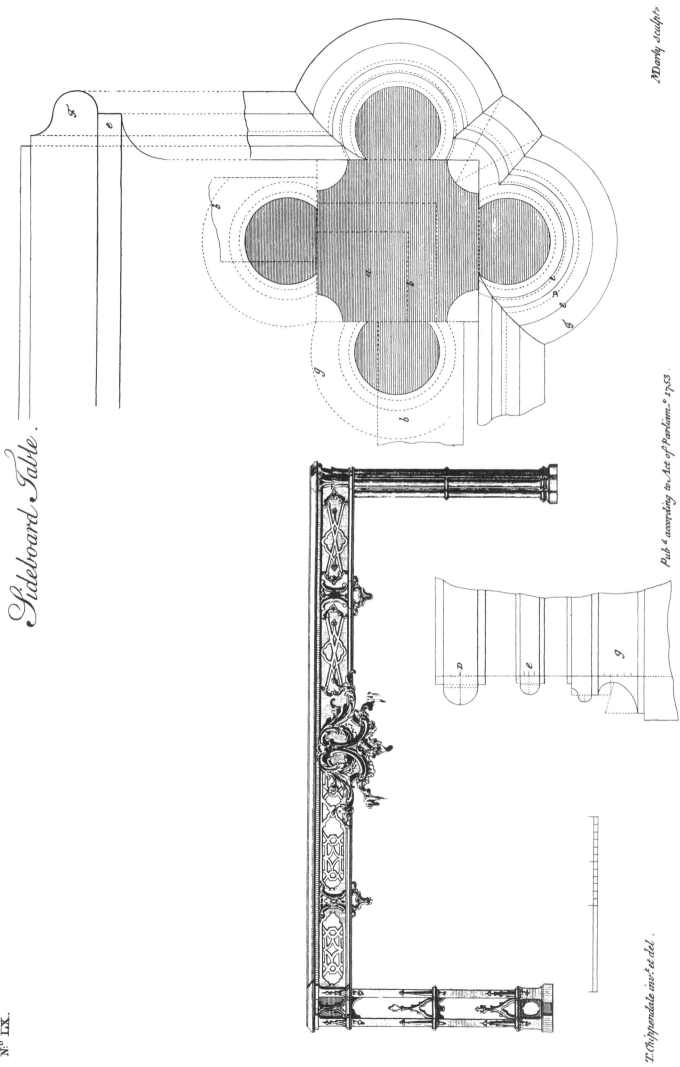

N.º IX.

Sideboard Table.

T. Chippendale inv.t et del.

Pub.d according to Act of Parliam.t 1753.

MDarly sculp.r

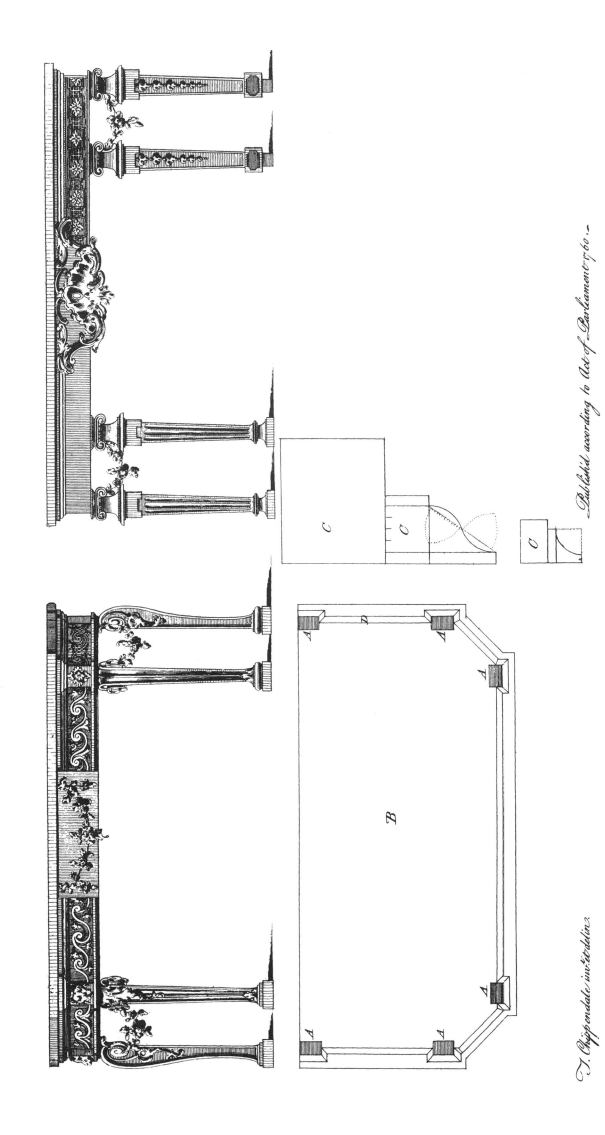

Sideboard Tables.

T. Chippendale inv. et delin.

Published according to Act of Parliament 1760.

Buroe Dressing Tables.

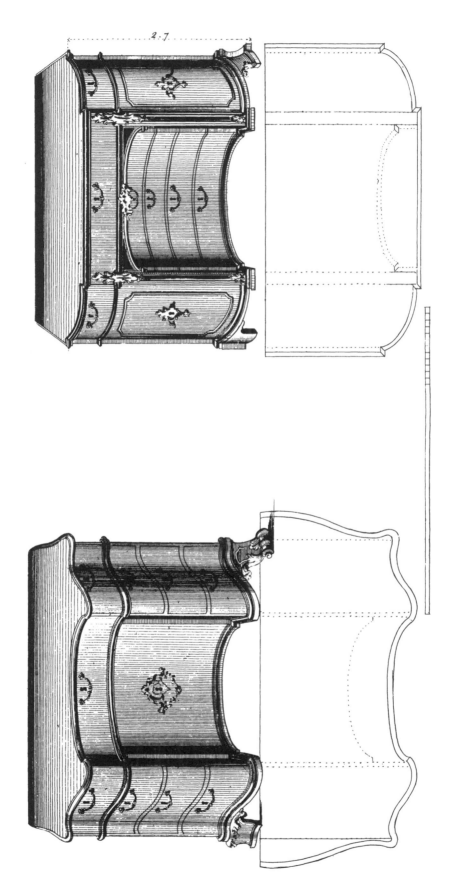

2.7

T.Chippendale inv. et delin.

Publish'd according to Act of Parliament 1760.

Buroe Dressing Tables.

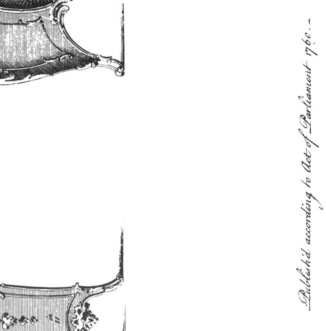

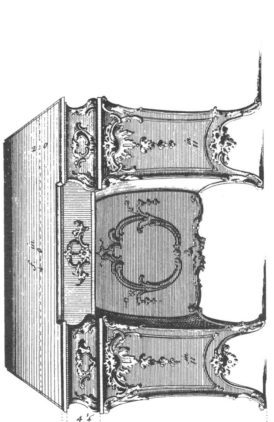

T. Chippendale inv.t et delin.

Publish'd according to Act of Parliament 1760.

French Commode Table.

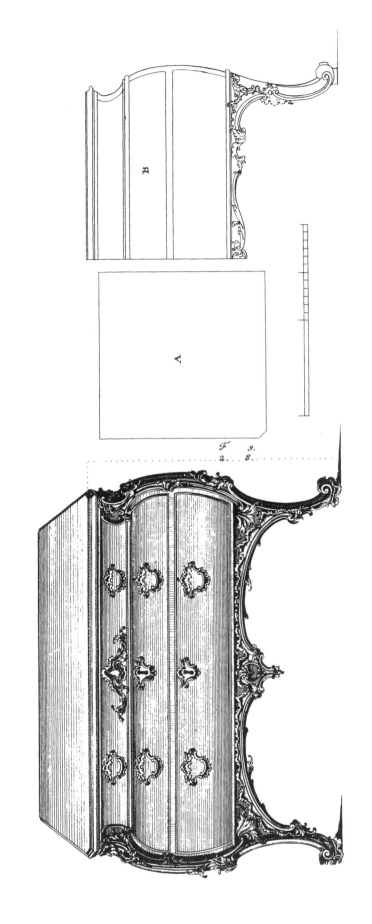

T. Chippendale inv.t et del.t

Publ.d according to Act of Parliam.t 1753

A Darly sculpt

French Commode Table.

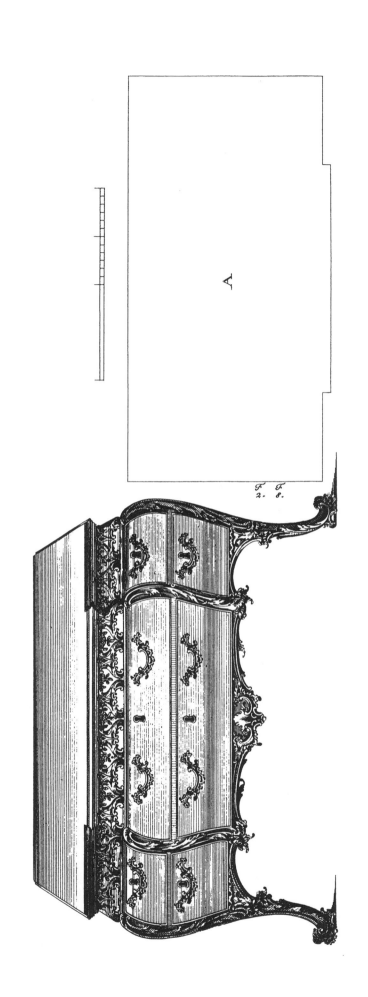

A

F F
2. 8.

T. Chippendale invt. et delt.

Publd. according to Act of Parliamt. 1753

T. Darly sculpt.

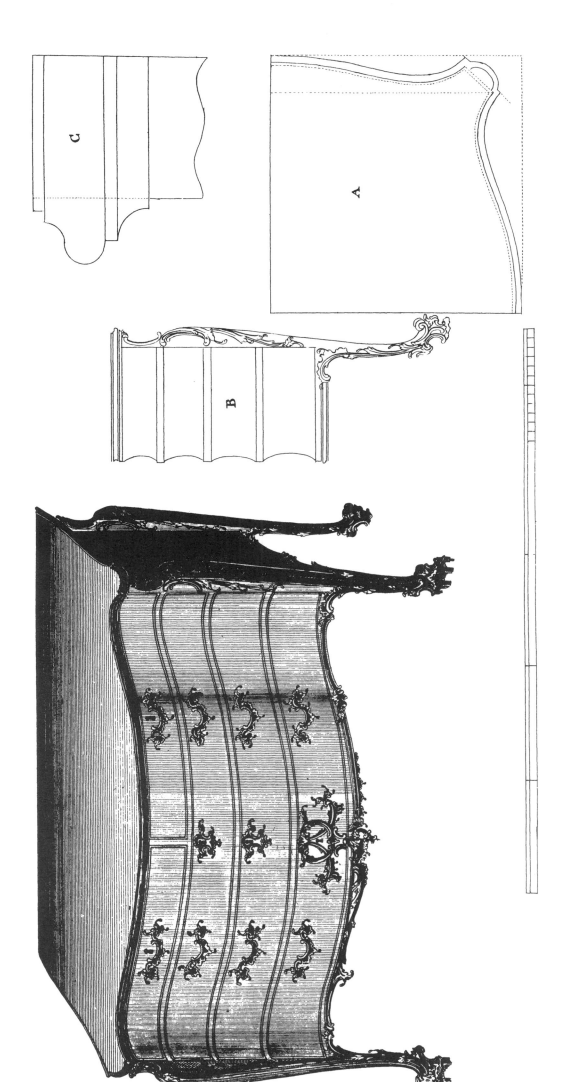

French Commode Table.

Nº LXVI.

C

B

A

T. Müller sculp.ᵗ

Pub.ᵈ according to Act of Parliamᵗ 1753

T. Chippendale invᵗ et del

Two Designs of Commode Tables.

T. Chippendale inv.t et delin.

Published according to Act of Parliam.t 1762.

Darly Sculp.

A French Commode.

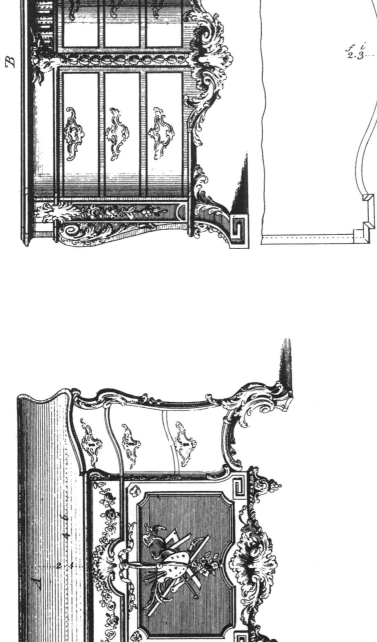

B

f i
2.3

2 . 10

T. Chippendale inv. et delin.

Published according to Act of Parliament 1762.

Darly Sculp.

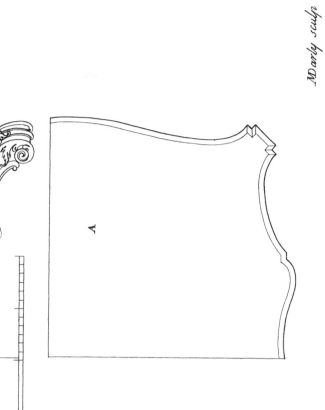

B

A

French Commode Table

T Chippendale inv.t et del.t

Pub.d accord.g to Act of Parl.t 1753

MDarly sculp.t

Commode Tables.

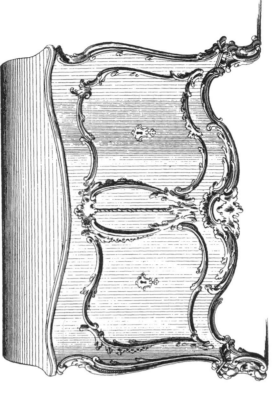

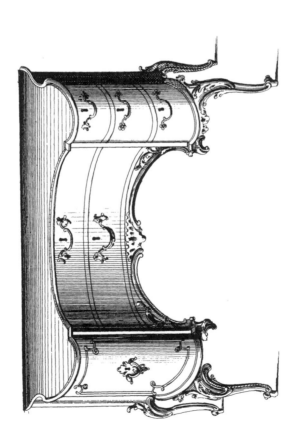

T Chippendale inv.t et delin x

Publish'd according to Act of Parlement 1760.

Darly Sculp.

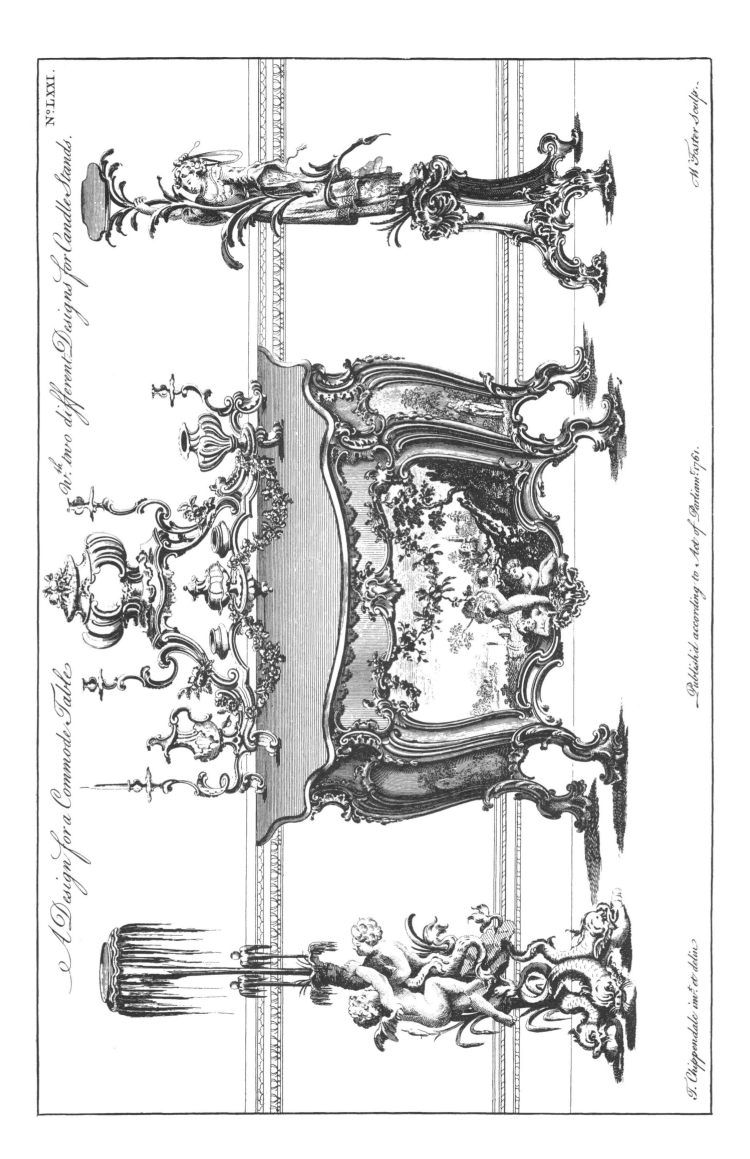

N.º LXXI.

A Design for a Commode Table

W.th two different Designs for Candle Stands.

T. Chippendale inv.t et delin.

Publish'd according to Act of Parliam.t 1761.

M. Foster Sculp.

A Writing Table

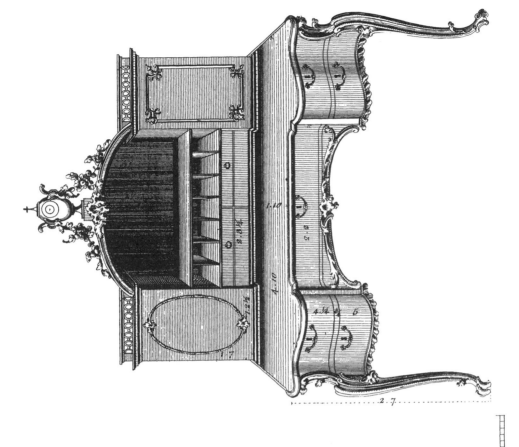

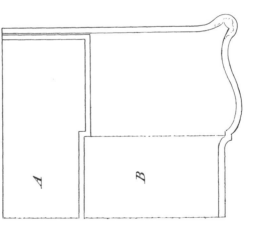

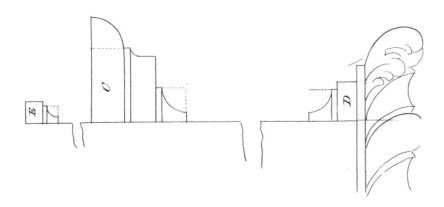

Publish'd according to Act of Parliament 1760.

T. Chippendale inv.t et delin.

Writing Table

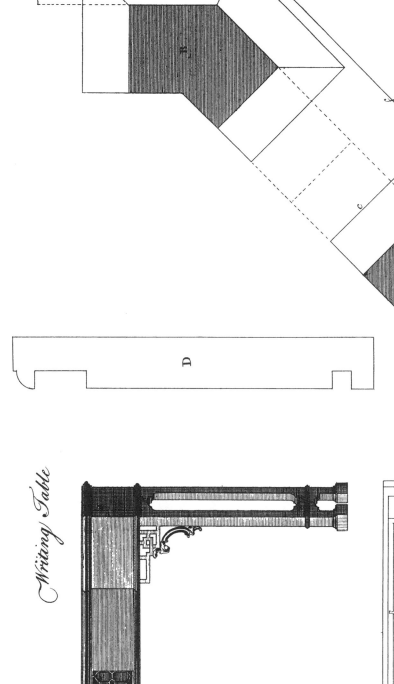

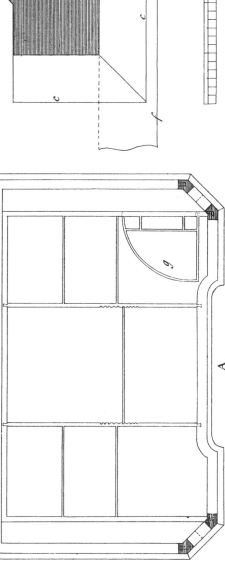

T. Chippendale inv.' et del.

Pub.' according to Act of Parliam.' 1753.

T. Müller sculp.

Writing Table.

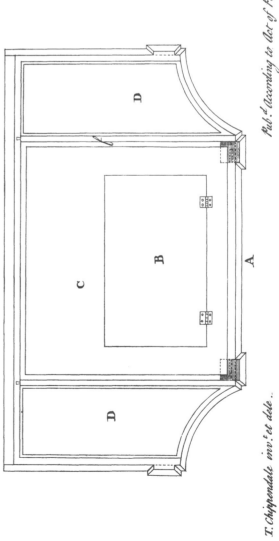

T. Chippendale inv.t et delin..

Pub.d According to Act of Parliam.t 1753.

T. Müller sculp..

A Writing Table

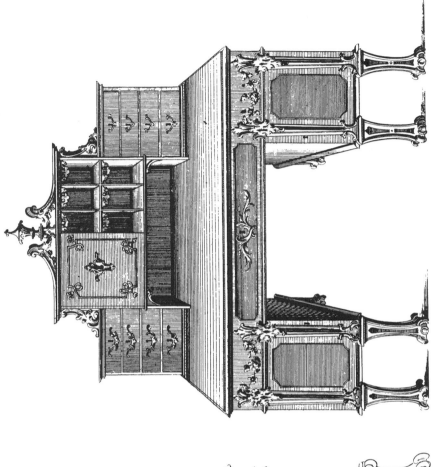

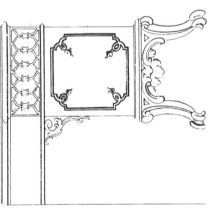

Published according to Act of Parliament. 1760.

T. Chippendale inv.t et delin.

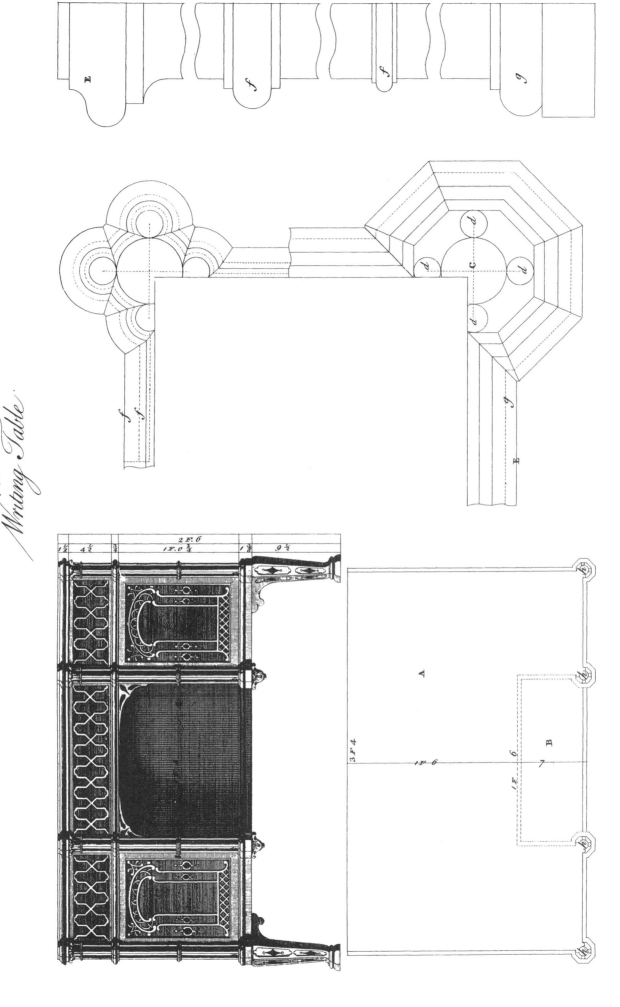

Writing Table.

T Chippendale inv: et del.

Pub according to Act of Parliam. 1753

I.S. Müller sculp.

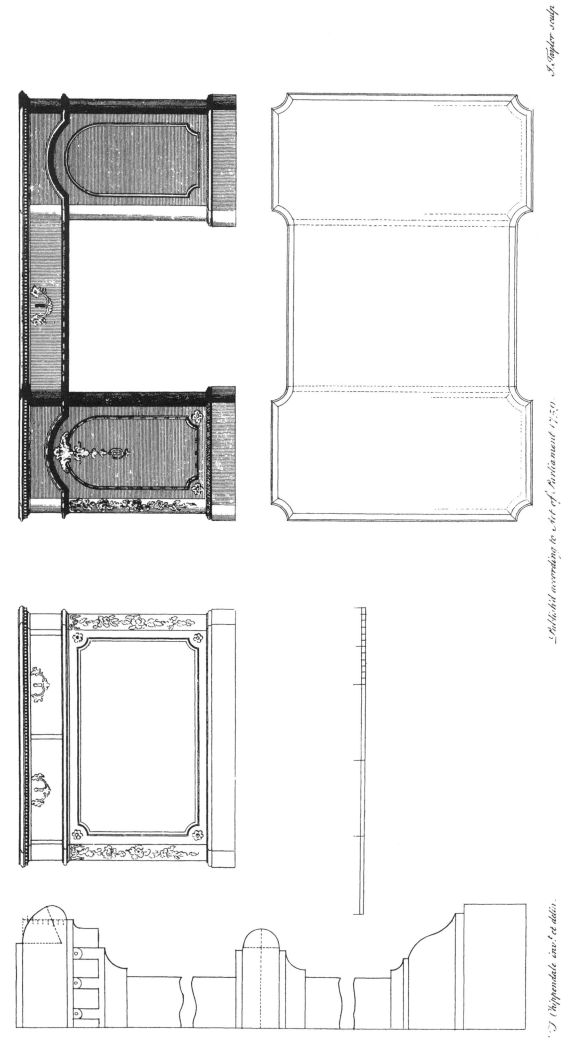

Library Tables —

Published according to Act of Parliament 1750.

T. Chippendale inv.t et delin.

I. Taylor sculp.

Library Table.

Pub.ª according to Act of Parliam. 1753

T. Chippendale inv. et del.

Library Table

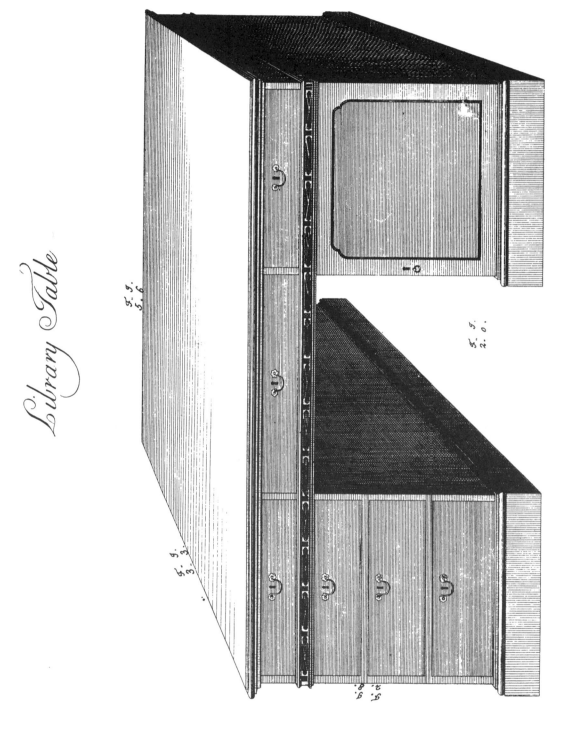

F. J.
5. 6.

F. J.
3. 3.

F. J.
2. 0.

F. J.
2. 8.

T. Chippendale inv. et delt.

Pub. according to Act of Parliam. 1753.

I. S. Miller sculp.

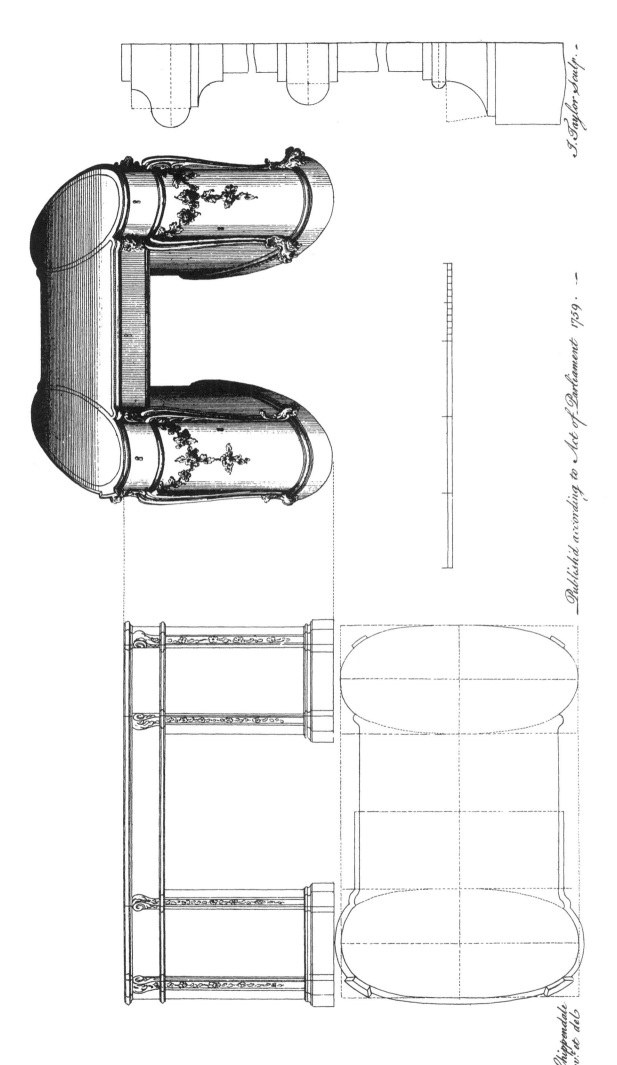

Library Table.

Published according to Act of Parliament 1759.

T. Chippendale
invt. et del.

I. Taylor sculp.

Library Table

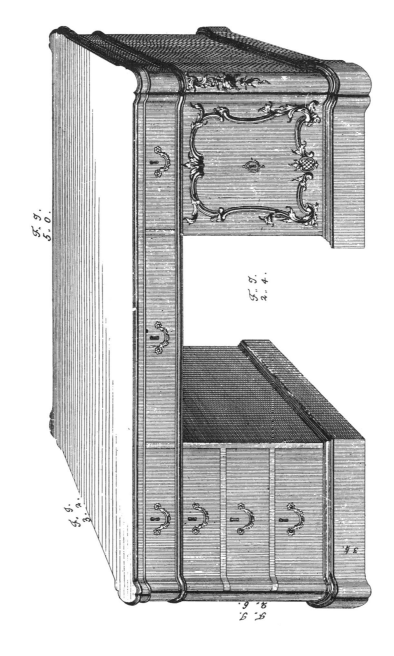

Fig.
5.0.

Fig.
2.4.

Fig.
2.3.

Fig.
2.6.

T. Chippendale inv.r et del.

Pub. according to Act of Parliam. 1753.

I. S. Müller sculp.

Library Table

T. Chippendale inv. et delin.

Publish'd according to Act of Parliament 1760.

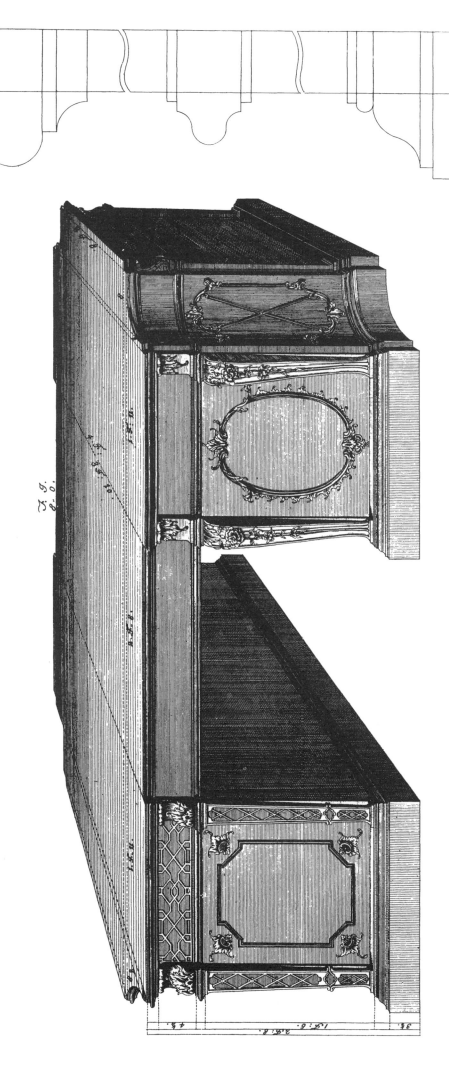

Library Table.

T. Chippendale inv. et del.

Publ. according to Act of Parliam.' 1753

T. Müller sculp.

Library Tables.

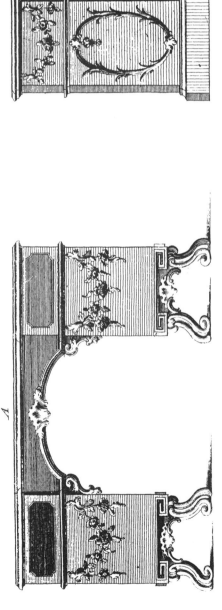

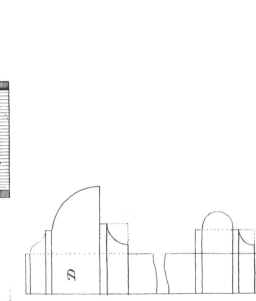

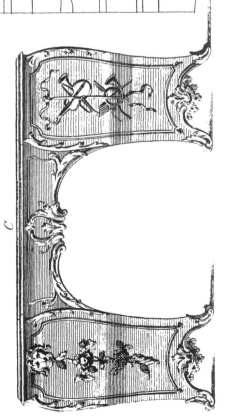

T. Chippendale invt. et del.

Published according to Act of Parliament 1760.

Library Table

F. I
8-0

F. I
4-0

F. I
1-1½

F. I
2-6

T. Chippendale inv. et del.

Pub. according to Act of Parliam. 1753.

J.S. Müller sculp.

Fig 1

9 8 7 6 5 4 3 2 1

9 8 7 6 5 4 3 2 1

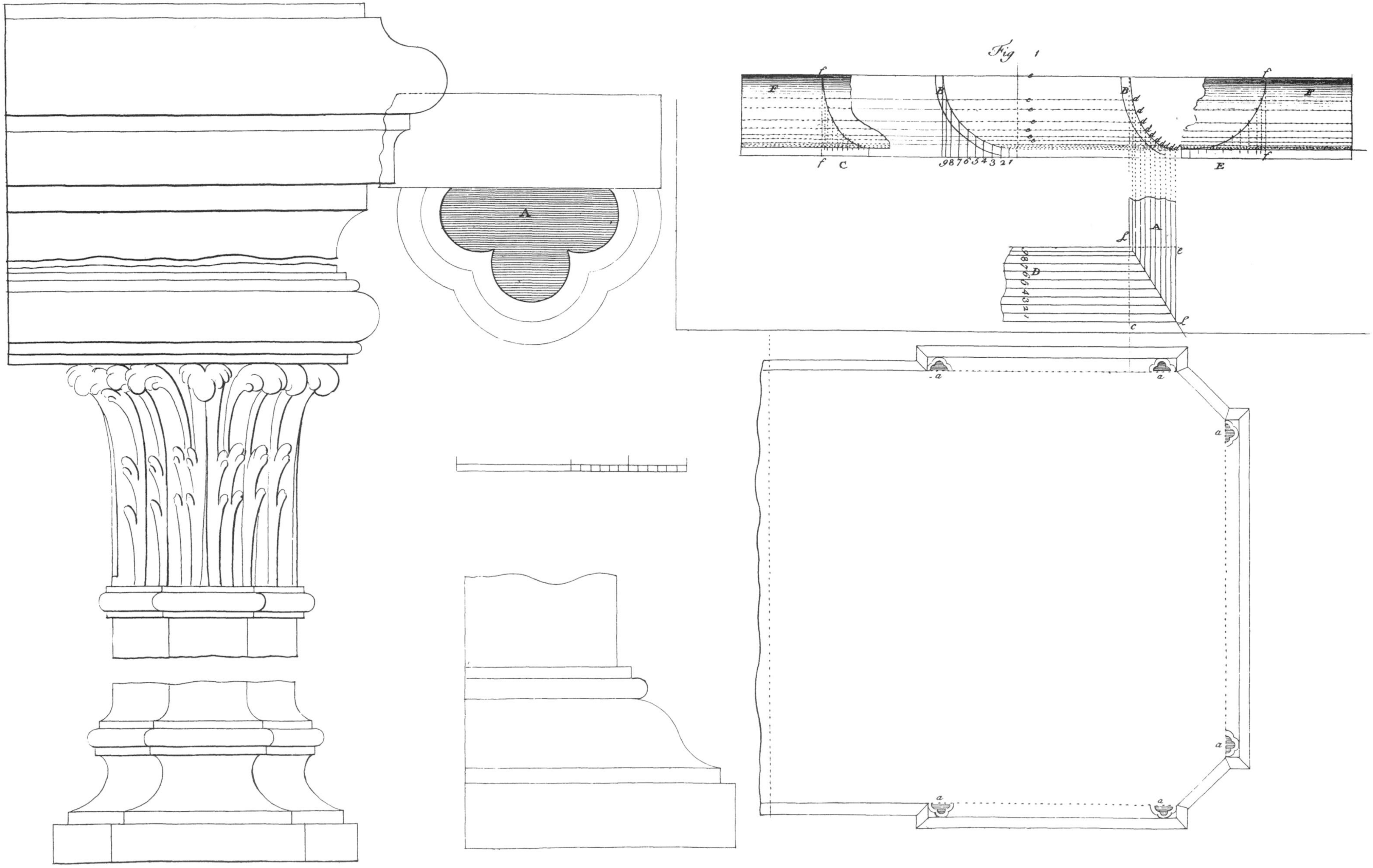

T. Chippendale inv.t et del.

Published according to Act of Parliament

M. Darly Sculp.

Two Bookcases.

T. Chippendale inv.t et delin.

Publish'd according to Act of Parliament 1759.

J. Taylor Sculp.

Two Library Bookcases.

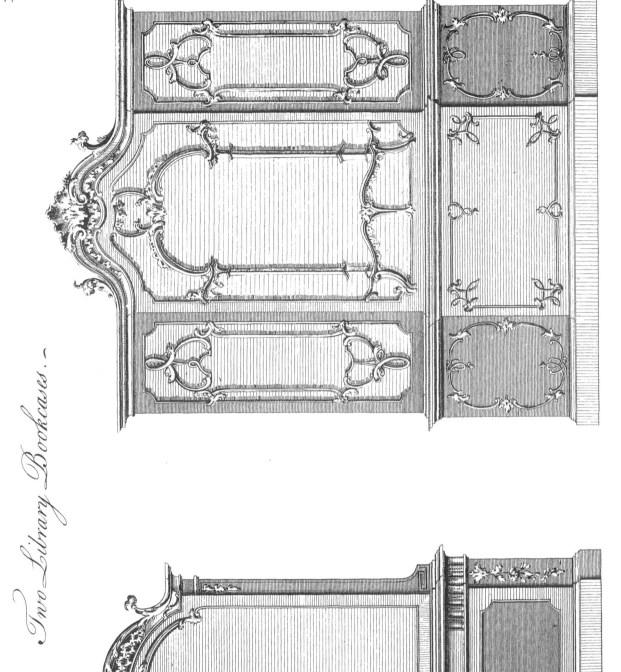

T. Chippendale inv.^t et delin.

Publish'd according to Act of Parliament 1760.

A Gothic Library Bookcase

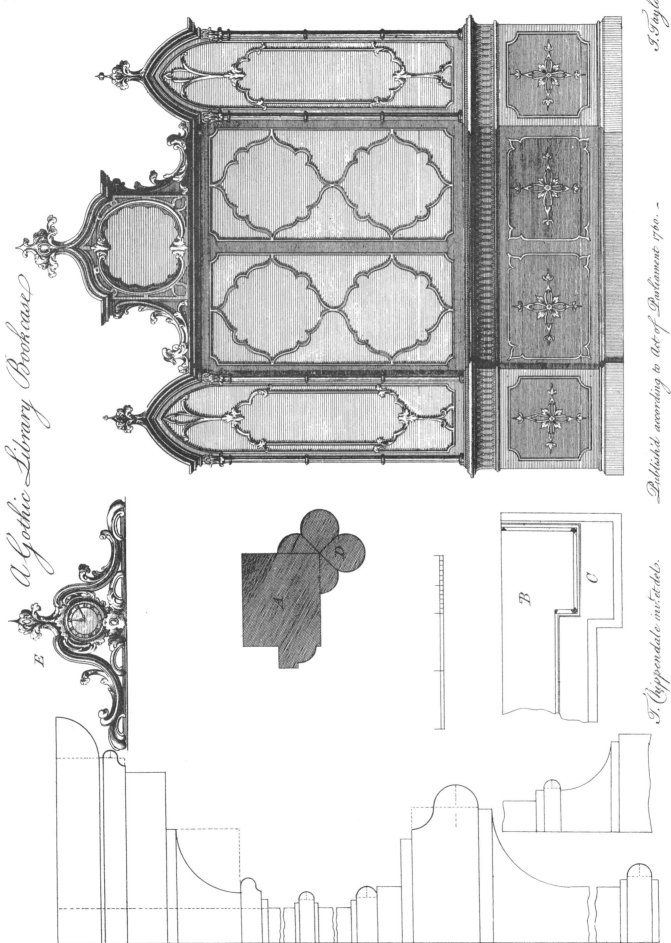

T. Chippendale inv: et del:

Publish'd according to Act of Parliament 1760.

I. Taylor Sculp.

Library Bookcase.

Fig 8

Fig 8

Fig 8

Fig 8

Fig 4

Fig 5

Publd according to Act of Parliam. 1753

T. Chippendale inv.t et del.

Library Bookcase.

T. Müller sculp.

Pubᵈ according to Act of Parliament 1753

T. Chippendale inv.ᵗ et del.

Plate XCII.

A Library Book-case.

T. Chippendale invt. et delin.

Published according to Act of Parliament 1760.

I. Taylor Sculp.

Library Bookcase

Pub: according to Act of Parliam.1753.

Chippendale inv. et del.

I.S. Müller sculp.

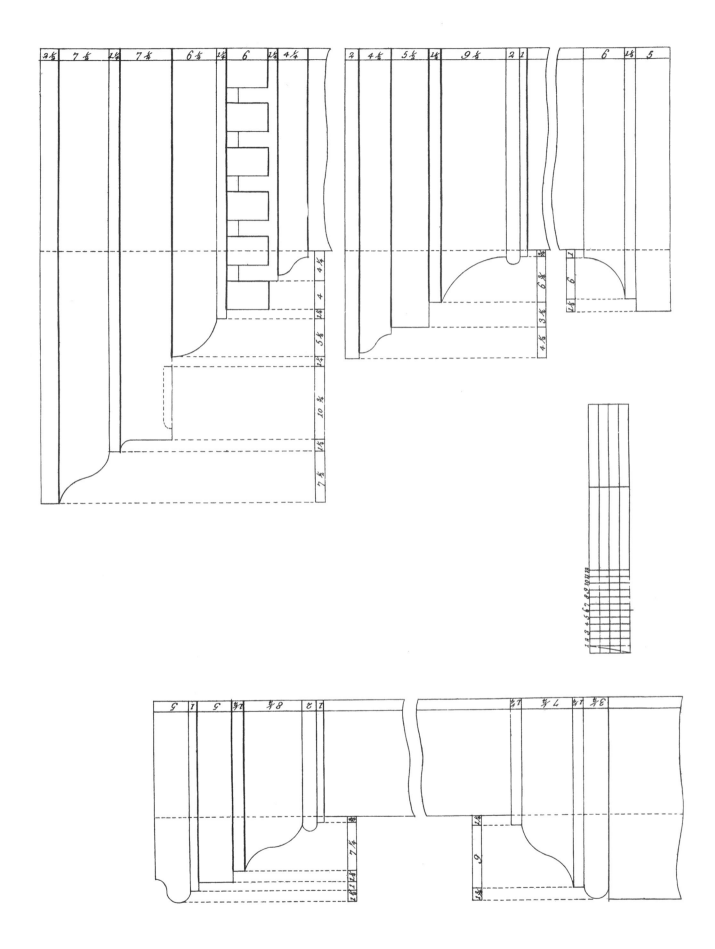

Library

Bookcase

I. S. Müller sculp.

Pub. according to Act of Parliam.r 1753.

T. Chippendale inv. et del.r

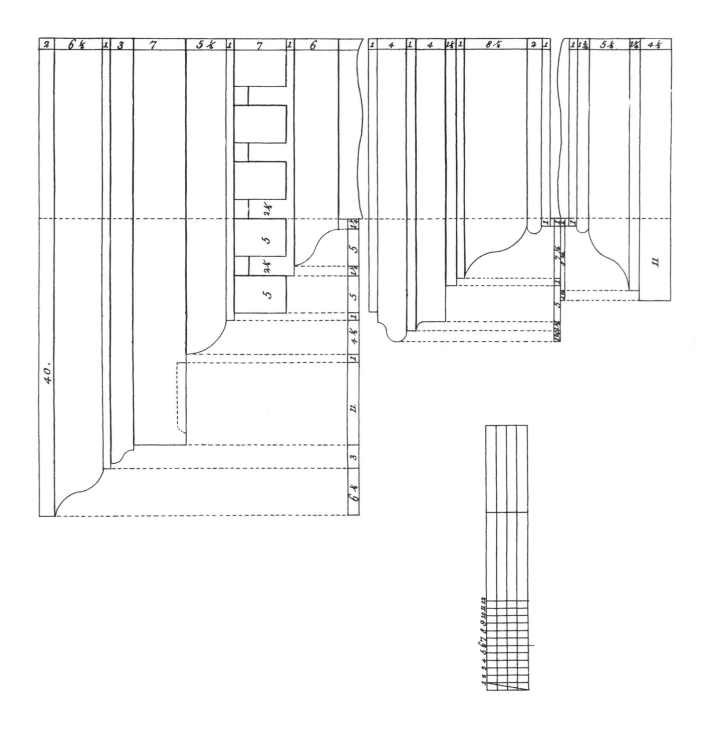

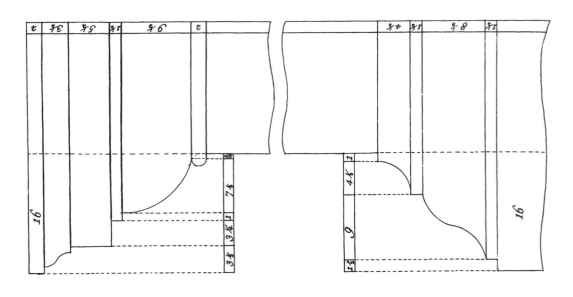

N.° XCVI

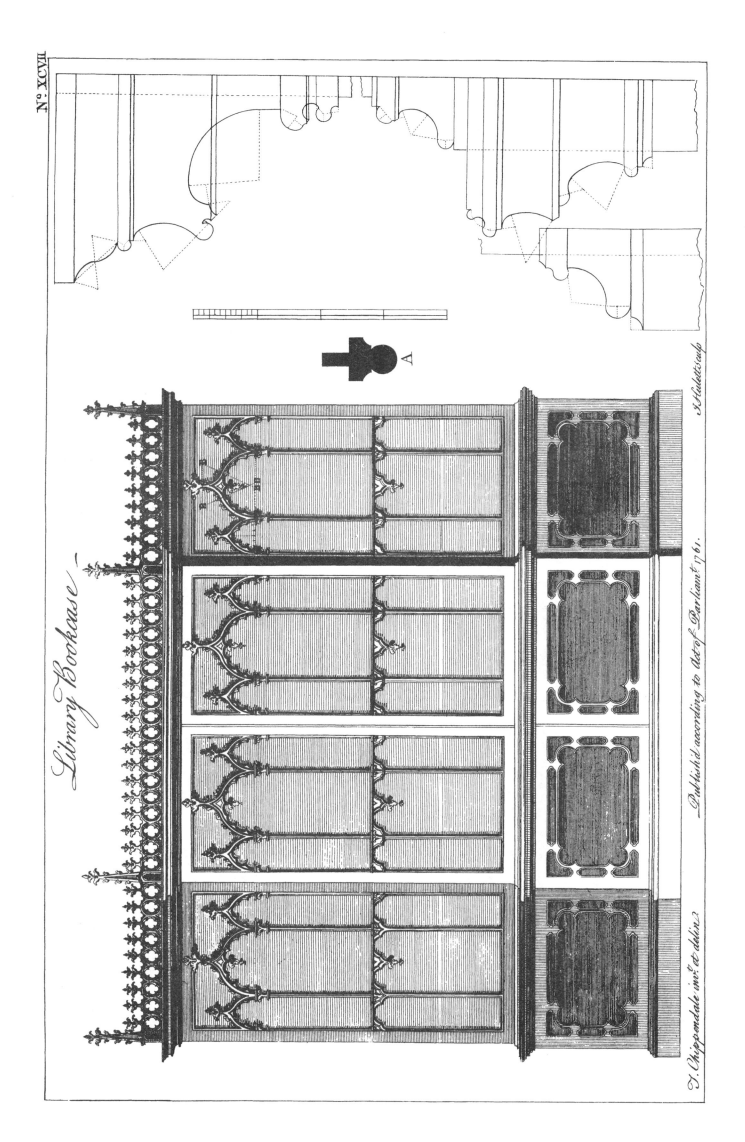

Library Bookcase

A

T. Chippendale inv:t et delin:.

Publish'd according to Act of Parliament 1761.

H. Hulett sculp

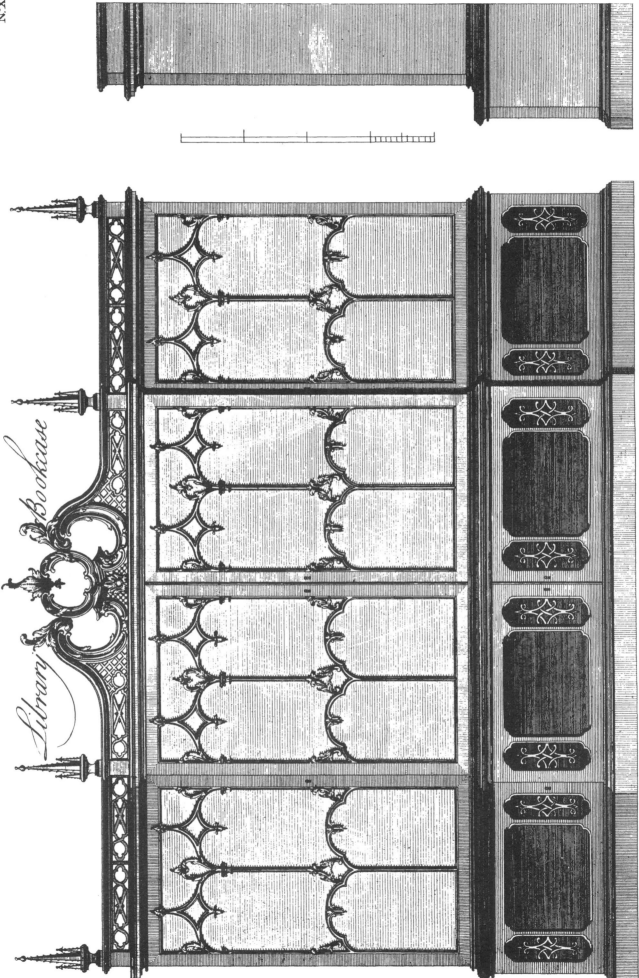

Library Bookcase

T. Chippendale inv. et del.

Pub. according to Act of Parliam. 1753

I.S. Müller sculp.

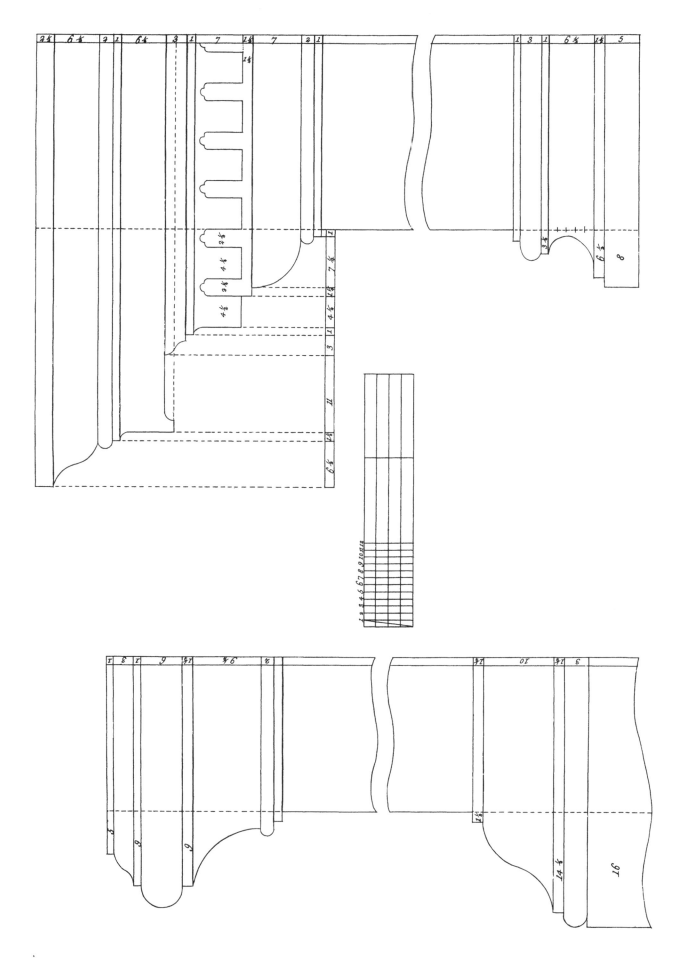

A Gothic Bookcase.

Published according to Act of Parliament 1761.

T. Chippendale inv.t et delin.

T. Miller sculp.

Library

Bookcase

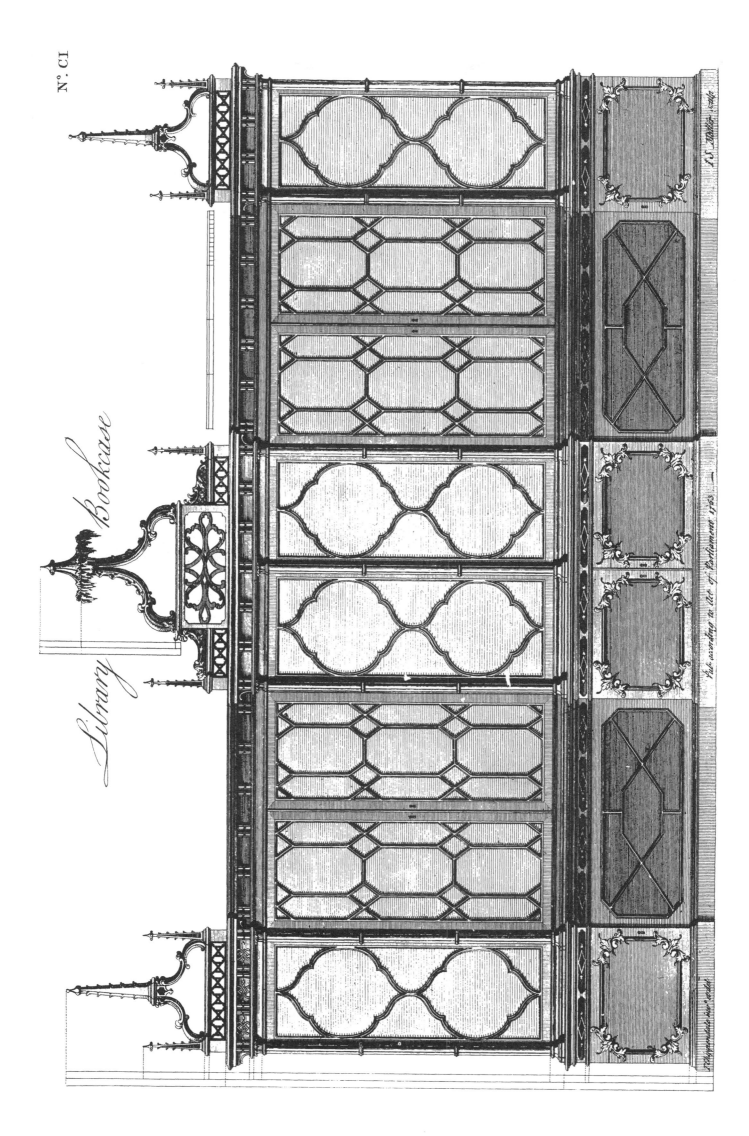

Published according to Act of Parliament 1753

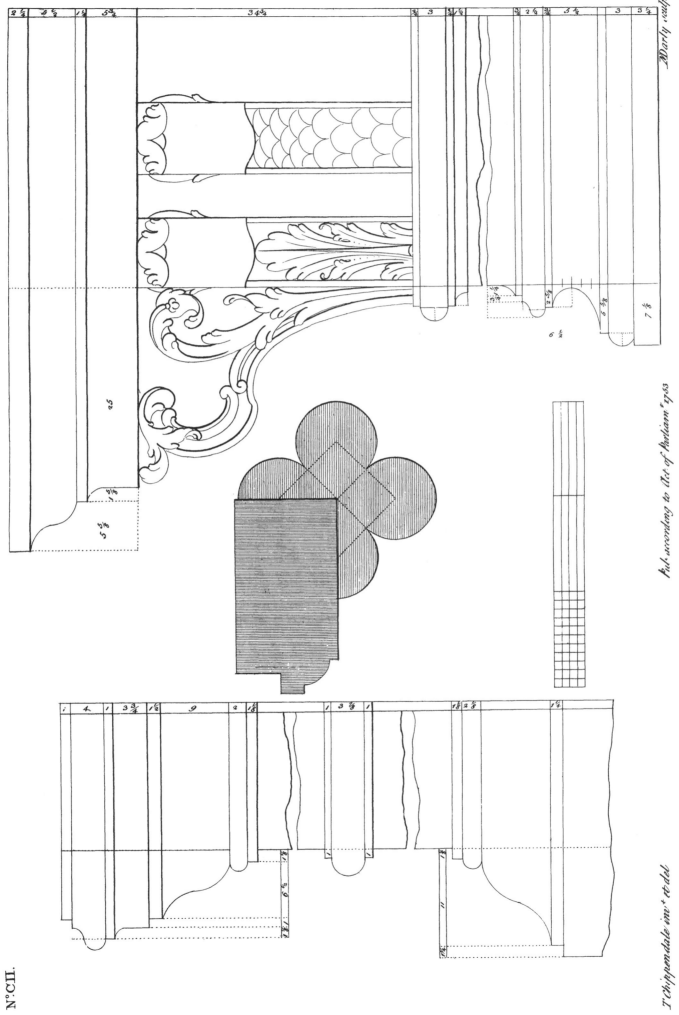

N.º CII.

T. Chippendale inv.t et del.

Pub. according to Act of Parliam.t 1753

Darly sculp.t

Chamber Organs.

T. Chippendale inv.et delin.

Published according to Act of Parliament 1761.

Hemerich sculp.

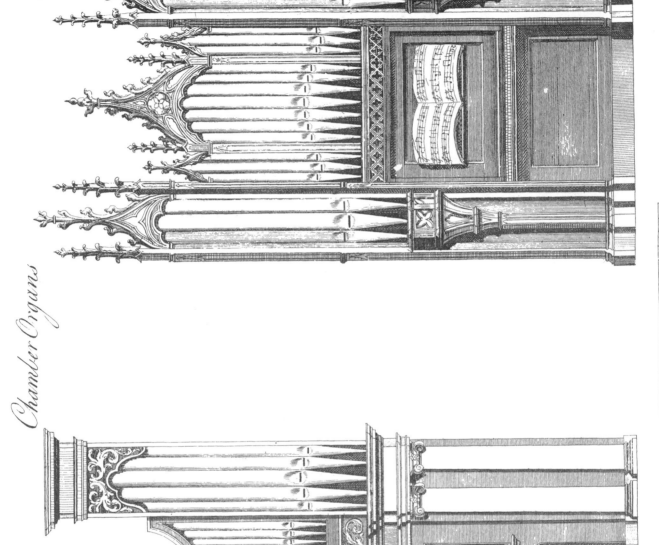

Chamber Organs

T. Chippendale inv. et delin

Published according to Act of Parliamt. 1760.

An＿*Organ*

T. Chippendale invᵗ et delin.   Publish'd according to Act of Parliamᵗ 1760.

A Gothic Organ

I. Chippendale invt. et delin.

Publish'd according to Act of Parliamt. 1761.

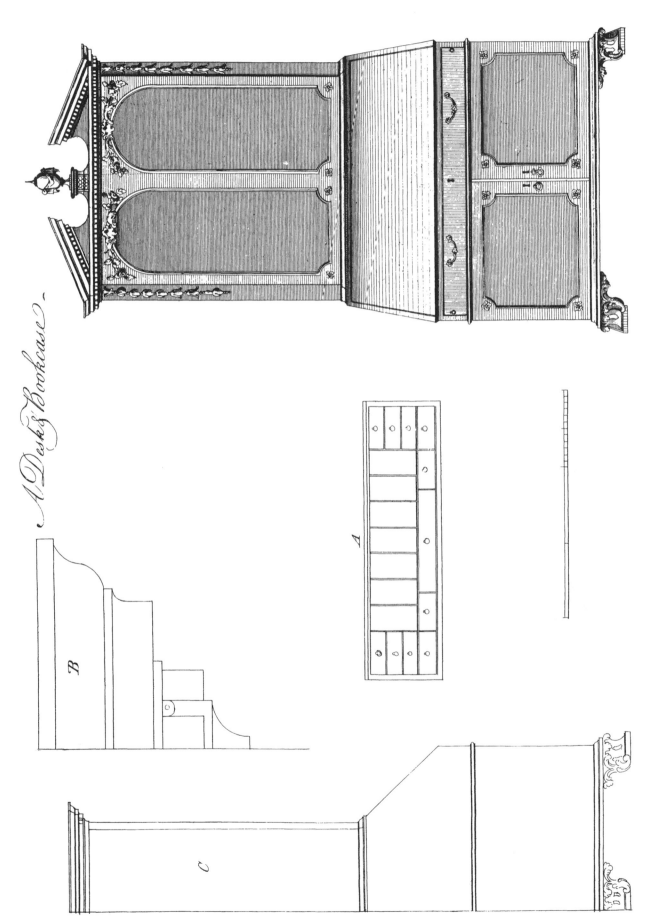

A Desk & Bookcase.

A

B

C

Published according to Act of Parliament 1760.

T. Chippendale inv.t et delin.

Desk & Bookcase.

T. Chippendale inv et delin.   Publish'd according to Act of Parliament   I.S. Müller Sculp.

Desk & Bookcase.

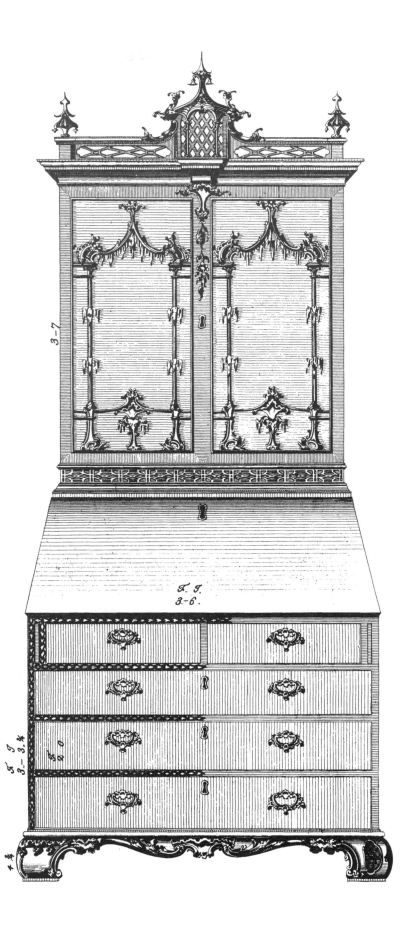

T. Chippendale inv.ᵗ et del.

Pub. according to Act of Parliam.ᵗ 1753

M.Darly sculp.

Desk & Bookcase

T. Chippendale inv. et del Pub.ᵈ according to Act of Parliament 1753 M. Darly sculp

Desk & Bookcase

T. Chippendale inv.^t et delin.   Publish'd according to Act of Parliament 1760.   M Darly sculp.

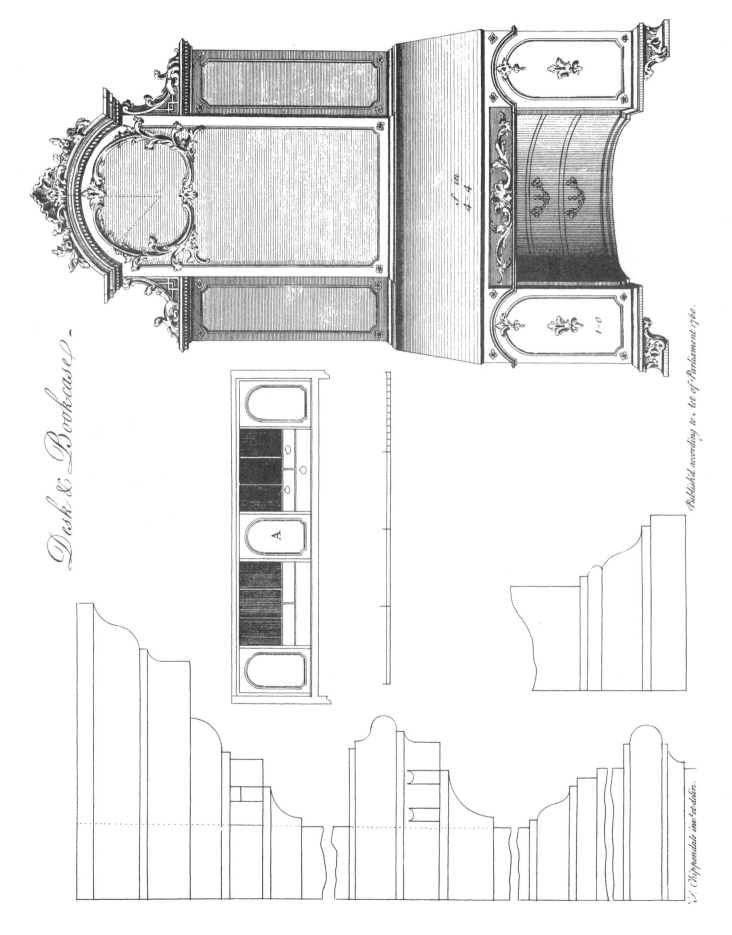

Desk & Bookcase.

A

Published according to. Act of Parliament 1760.

A. Darly sculp.

T. Chippendale inv. et delin.

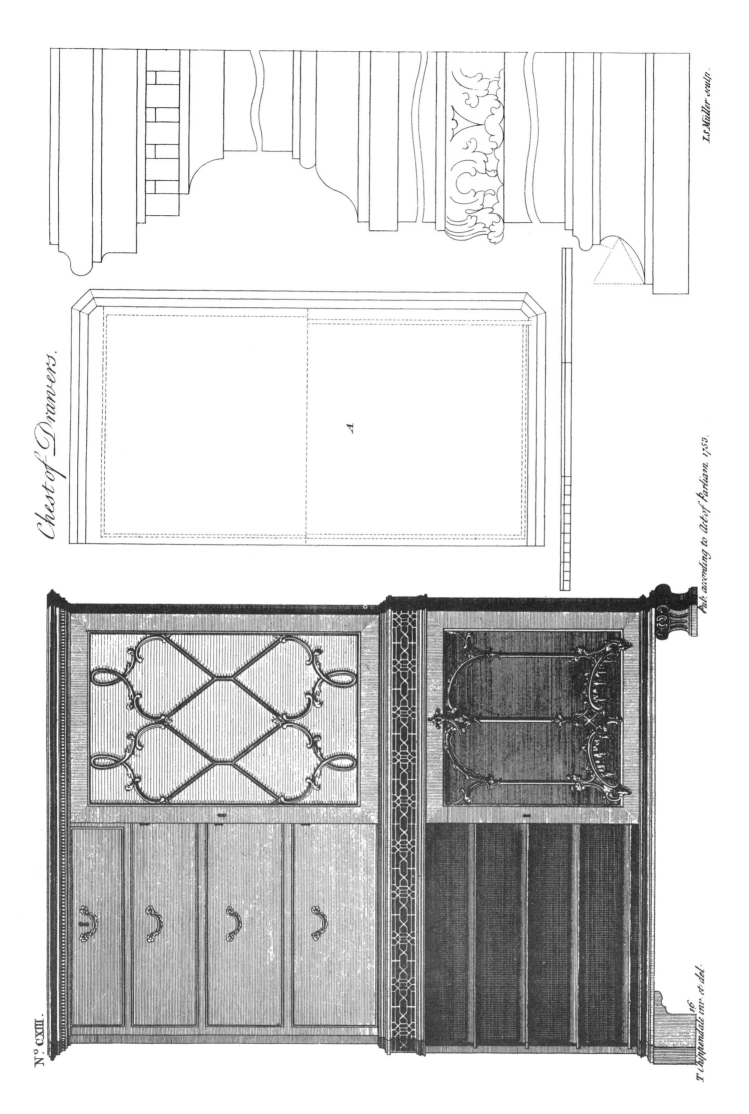

No. CXIII.

Chest of Drawers.

A

T. Chippendale inv. et del.

I.S. Müller sculp.

Pub. according to Act of Parliam. 1753.

16

Dressing Chest & Bookcase.

T. Chippendale inv.t et del.t.

Publ.t according to Act of Parliam.t 1753

M. Darly sculp.

Dressing Chest & Bookcase.

T. Chippendale inv. et del.

Pub. according to Act of Parliam'. 1753.

T. Darly sculp.

A Ladys Writing Table & Book-case

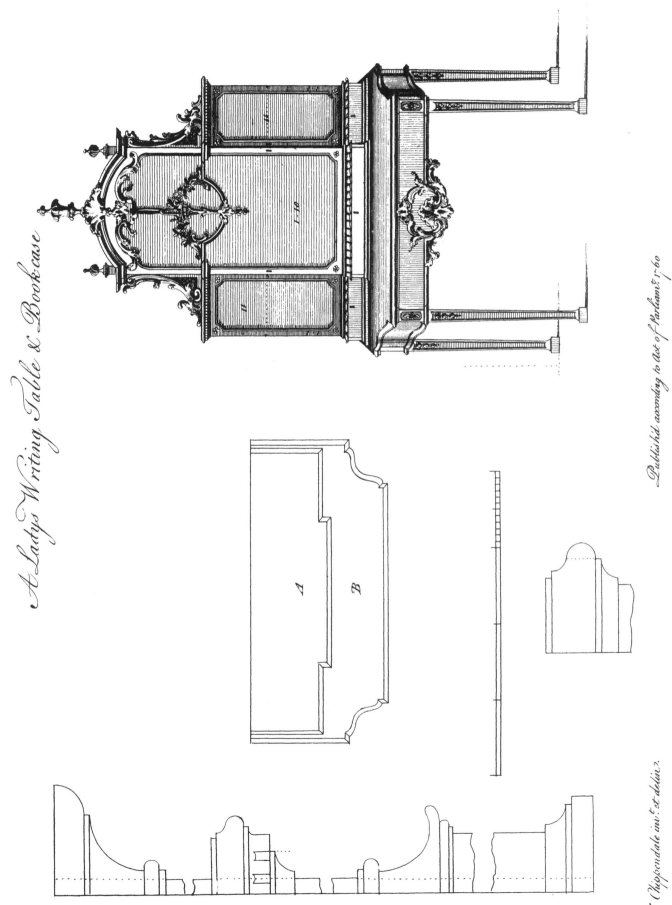

T. Chippendale invᵗ et delinᵗ.   Published according to Act of Parliamᵗ 1760.   Darly Sculp.

A Ladies Writing Table & Bookcase

Chipendale inv.t et delin.

Publsh'd according to Act of Parliam.t 1760.

Darly Sculp.

Design for a *Toylet Table*

T. Chippendale invt. et delin.   Publish'd according to Act of Parliamt. 1761.   W. Foster Sculp.

A Toylet Table

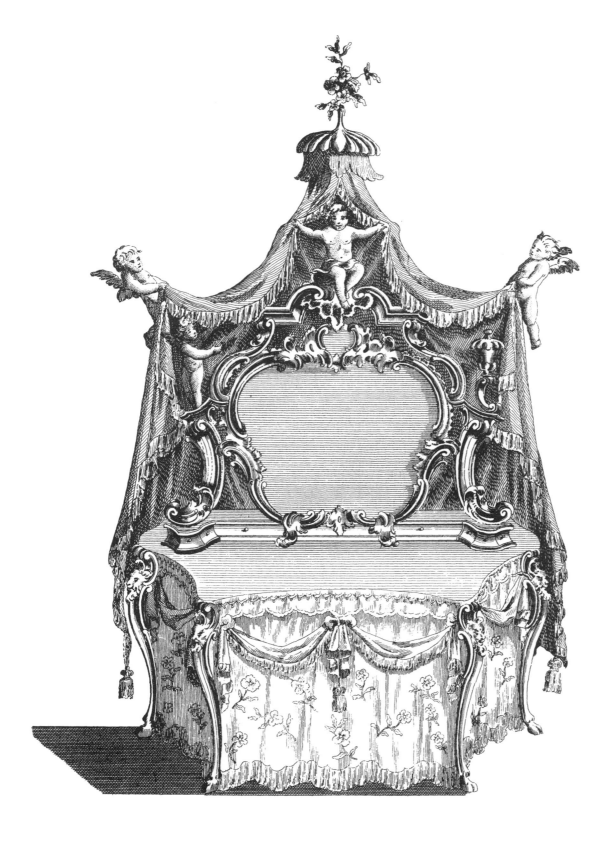

T. Chippendale inv.ᵗ et delin.ᵗ   Publish'd according to Act of Parliament 1760.   Morris sculp.

Cabinet

T. Chippendale inv.t et del.

Pub.d according to Act of Parliam. 1753.

T. Miller sculp.

Cabinet.

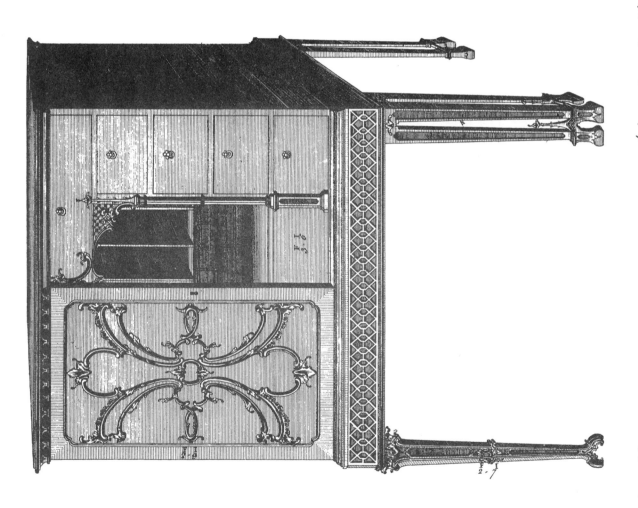

T. Chippendale inv.t et del.

Pub.d according to Act of Parliam.t 1753.

T. Miller sculp.

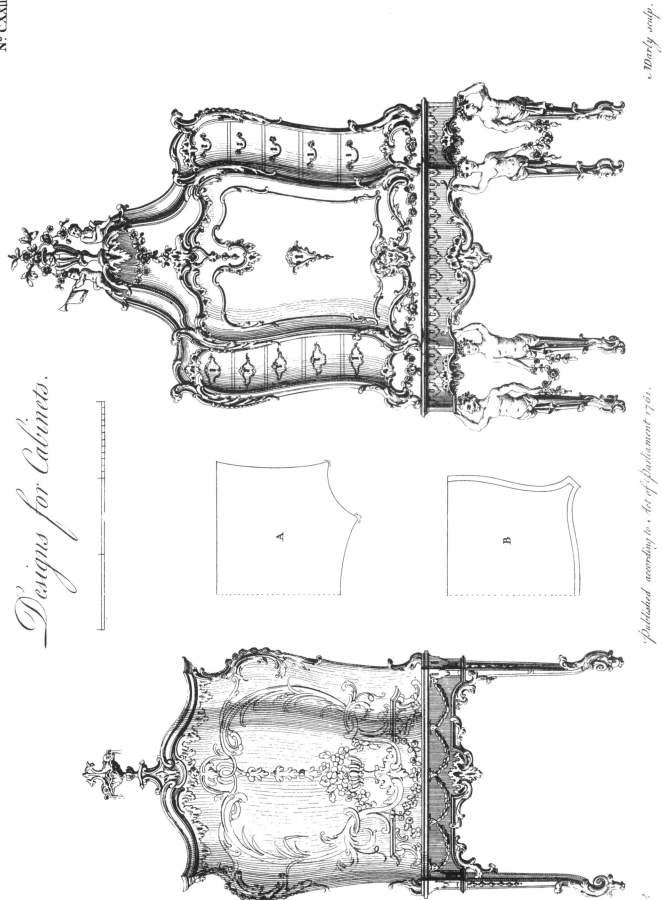

Designs for Cabinets.

A

B

J. Chippendale inv.t et delin.?

Published according to . Act of Parliament 1761.

I. Darly sculp.

N.° CXXIII

Chinese Cabinet.

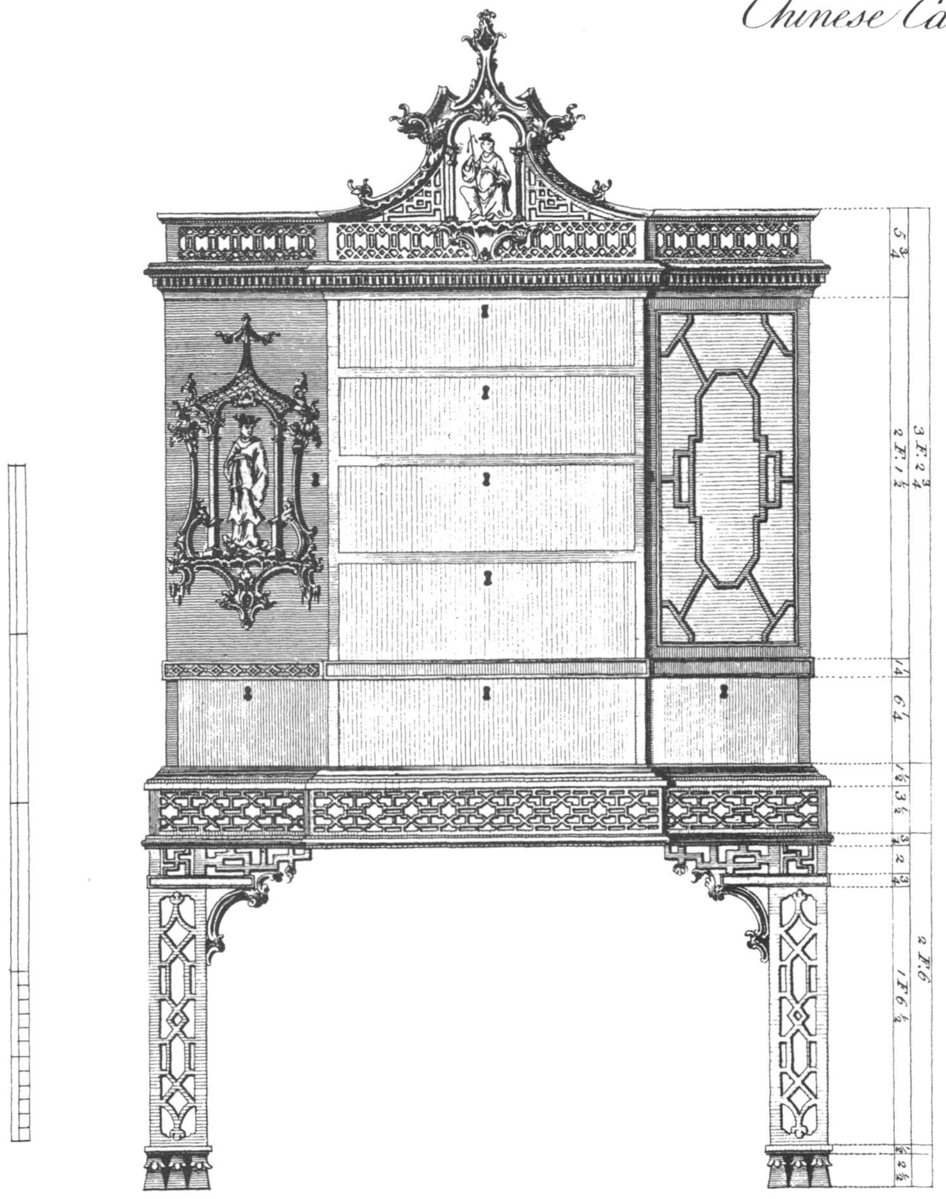

3 F. 2 3/4
5 3/4
2 F. 1 1/2
1/4
6 1/4
1 1/2
3 1/2
3/4
2
3/4
2 F. 6
1 F. 6 1/2
1/2
2 1/2

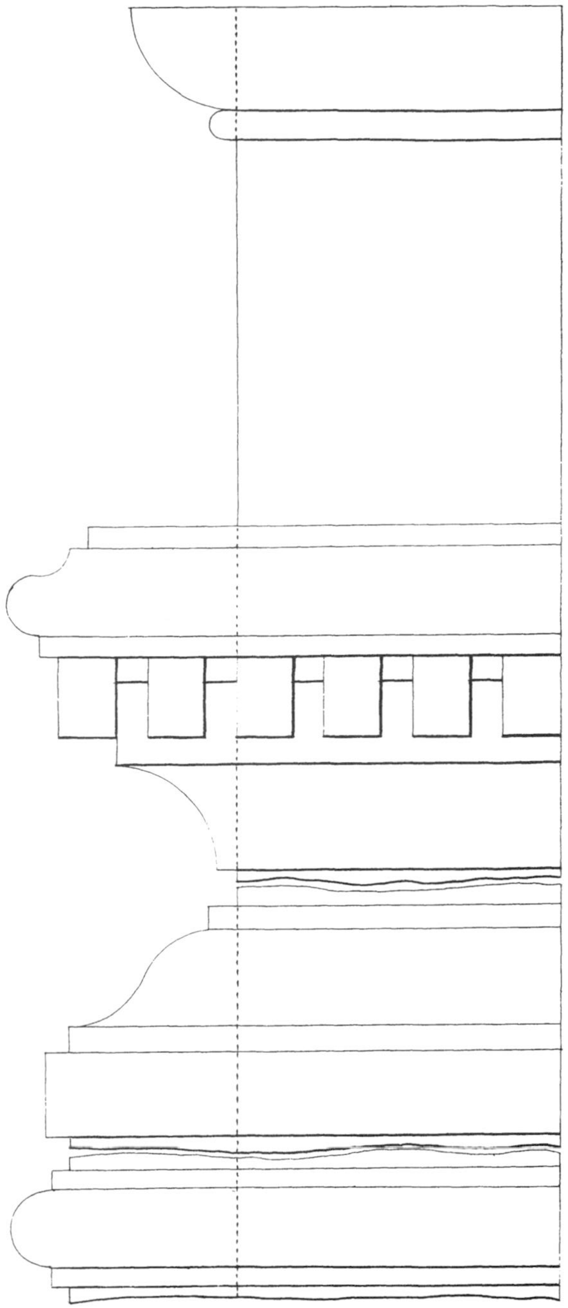

T. Chippendale inv. et delin.

Publish'd according to Act of Parliam.t

M. Darly Sculp.

A Cabinet.

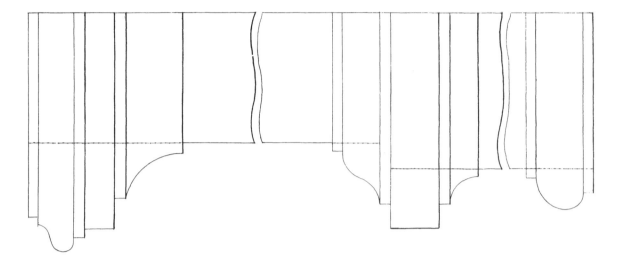

T. Chippendale invt et del.

Published according to Act of Parliament

M. Darly Sculpt

Gothick Cabinet.

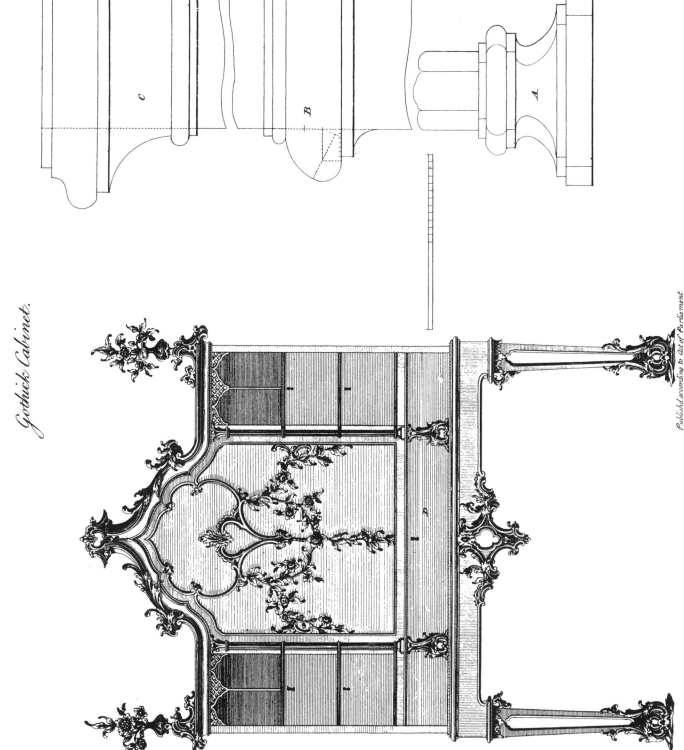

M. Darly Sculp.

Published according to Act of Parliament

T. Chippendale inv.t et del.

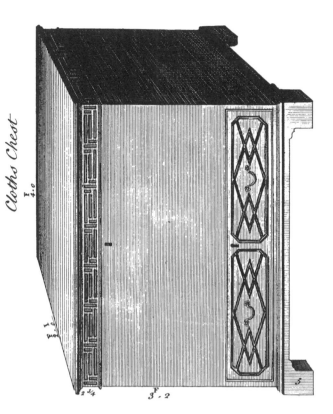

Cloths Chest
I.o
4.o

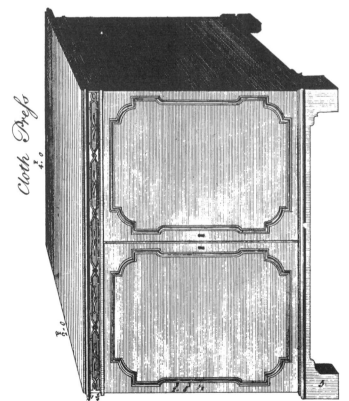

Cloth Press
I.o
4.o

T: Chippendale inv.t et del.

Pub.d according to Act of Parliam 1753

T: Müller sculp.

Gothick Cloths Chest.

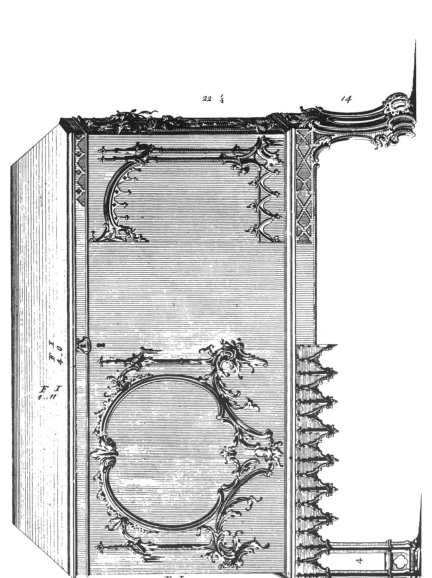

T. Chipendale inv.t & del.

Publ.d according to Act of Parliam.t 1753.

Darly sculp.

Two Designs of Cloths Chest

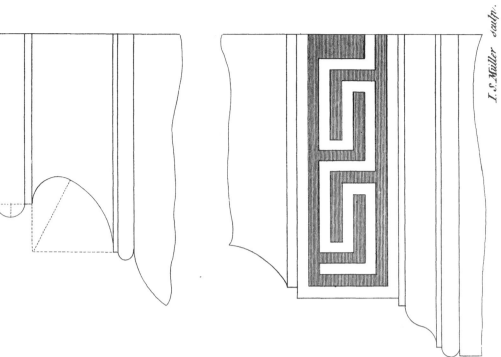

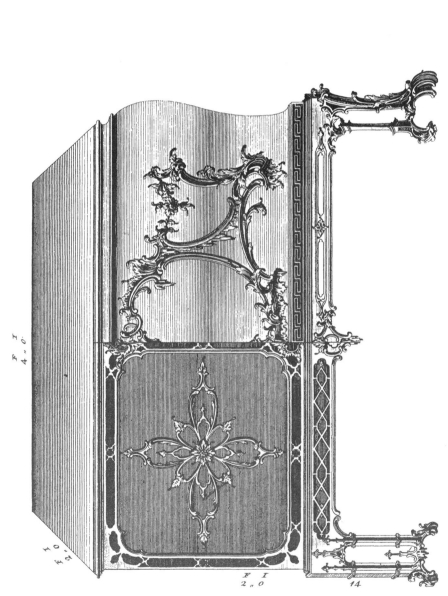

T. Chippendale inv. et del.

Pub. according to Act of Parliam. 1753.

I. S. Müller sculp.

Cloaths Prefs.

T. Chippendale inv.t et del.

Publ. according to Act of Parliam.t 1753.

I.M.Darly sculp.t

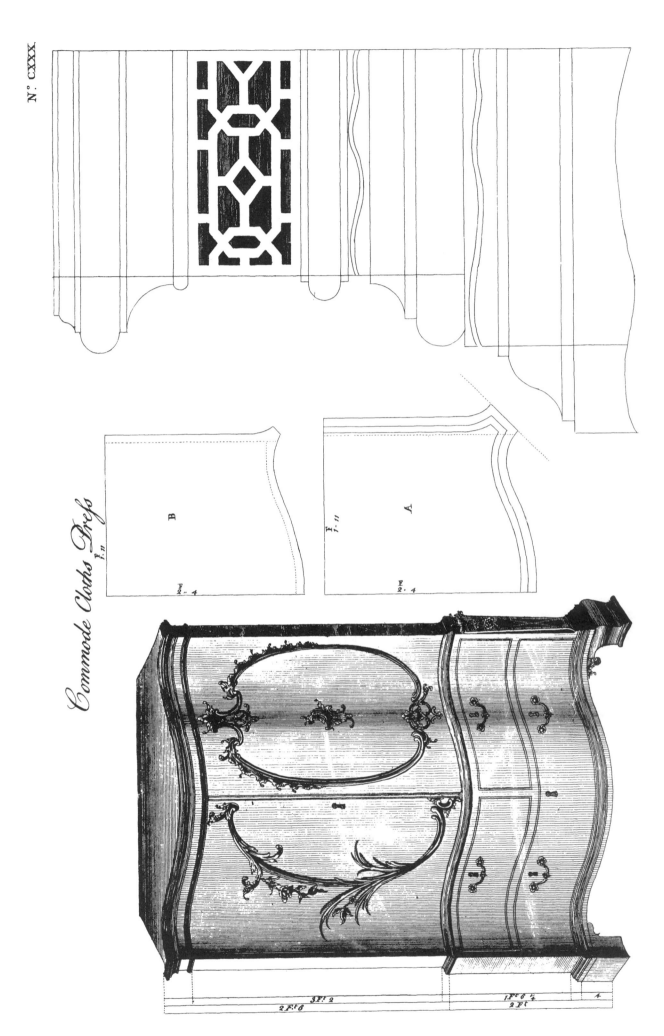

Commode Cloths Prefs

Pub.d according to Act of Parliam.t 1753

T. Chippendale inv.t et del.

T. Müller sculp.

Commode Cloths Prefs.

Publ. according to Act of Parliam. 1763.

T. Chippendale inv. et del.

J.S. Müller sculp.

China Case.

M. Darly Sculp.^r

T. Chippendale inv.^t et del.

Published according to Act of Parliament

China Gate.

T. Chippendale inv. et delin.

Publ. according to Act of Parliam. 1753.

J.S. Müller sculp.

China Case.

T. Chippendale invᵗ et del

Pub.ᵈ according to Act of Parliamᵗ 1753

M. Darly sculpᵗ

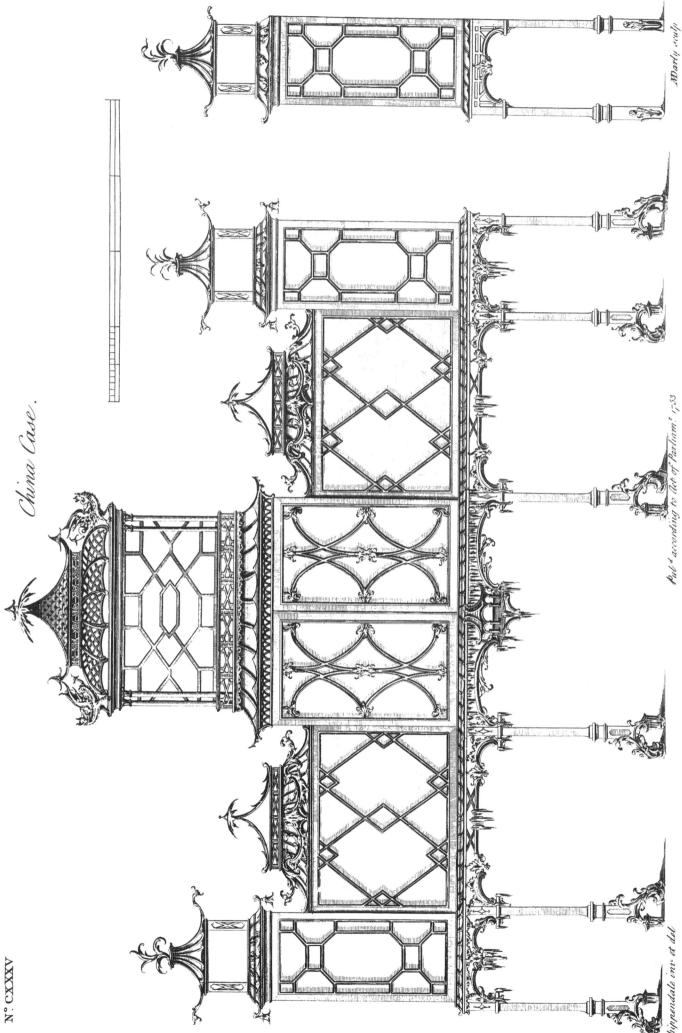

N.º CXXXV

China Case.

r. Chippendale inv.t et del.

Pub.d according to Act off Parliam.t 1753

T. Morris sculp

A China Case.

T. Chippendale invᵗ et delin.   Publish'd according to Act of Parliament 1760. —

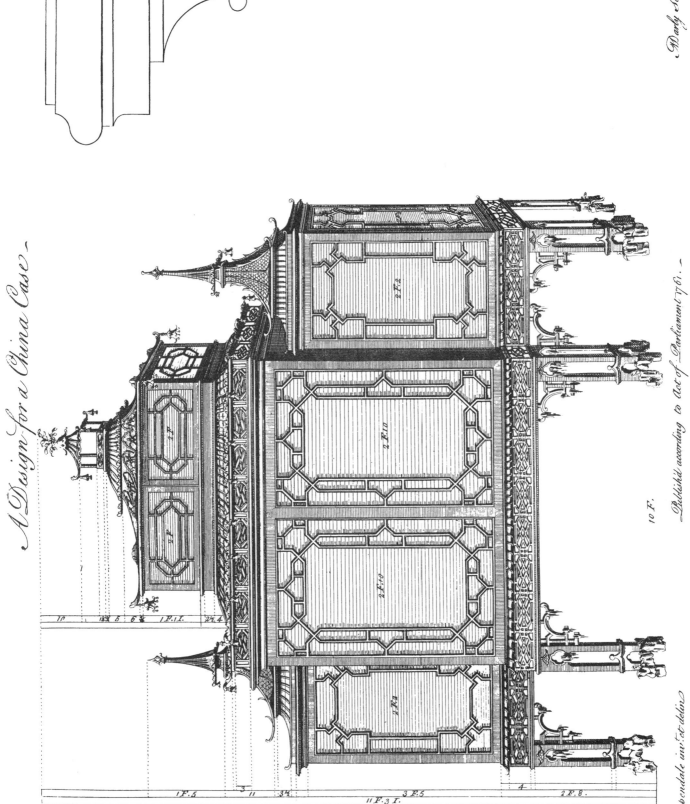

A Design for a China Case.

Nº. CXXXVII.

T. Chippendale inv.t et delin.

Published according to Act of Parliament 1761.

Darly sculp.

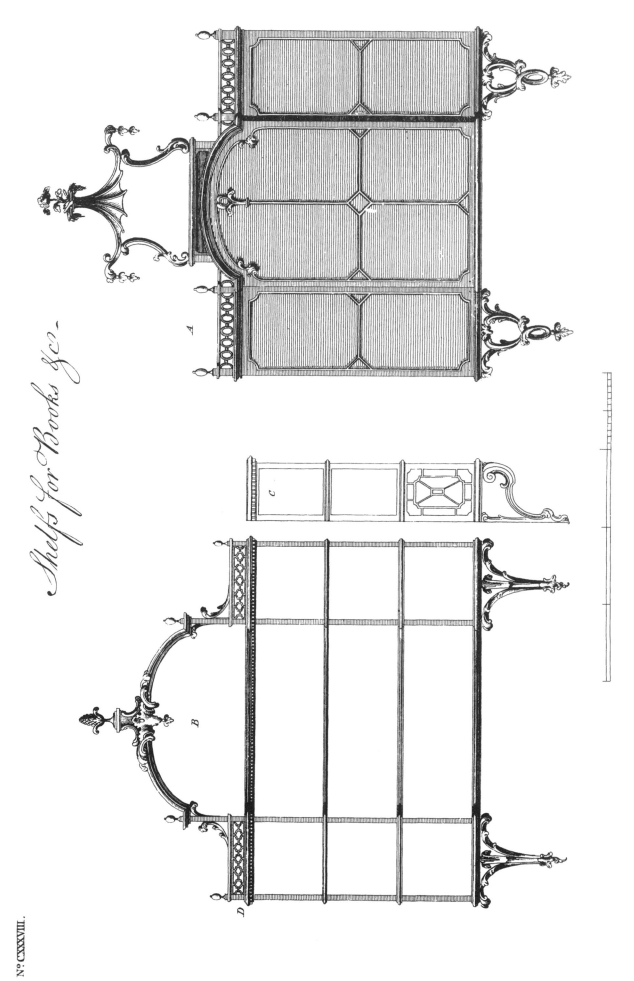

Shelfs for Books &c.

T. Chippendale inv.ᵗ et delin.

Published according to Act of Parliament.

T. Taylor sculp.

Hanging Shelves.

A

a

B

A

T. Chippendale invt. et del.

Published according to Act of Parliament

M. Darly Sculpt.

Hanging Shelves.

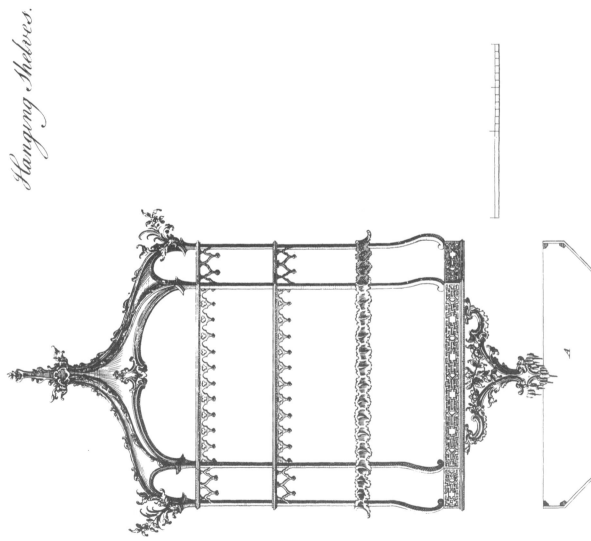

T. Chippendale inv. et del.

Publish'd according to Act of Parliament

M. Darly Sculp.

Shelves for China.

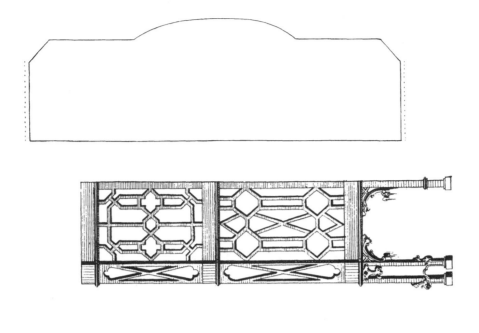

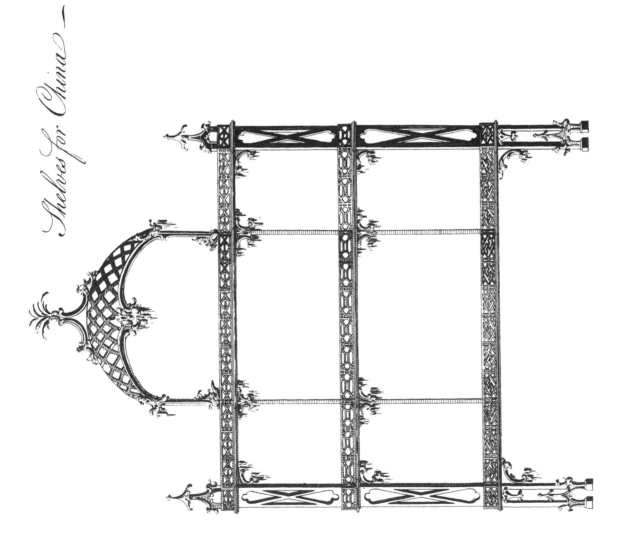

T. Chippendale inv. et delin.

Published according to Act of Parliament 761.

Darly sculp.

China Shelf.

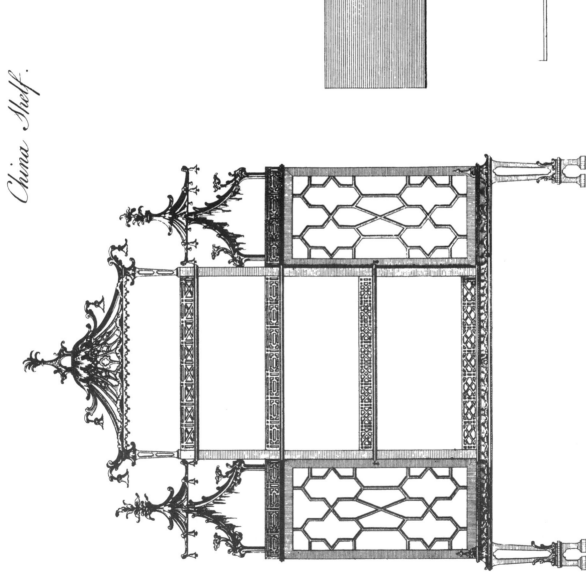

T. Chippendale inv. et delin.

Published according to Act of Parliament.

A. Darly Sculp.

Designs for China Shelves ~

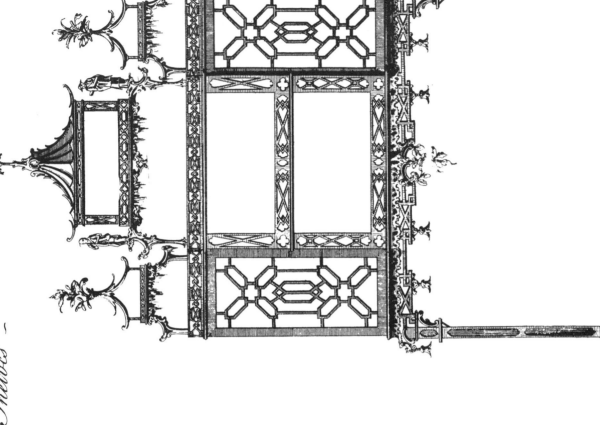

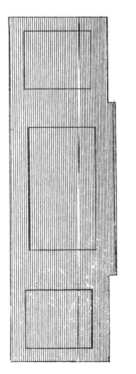

Published according to Act of Parliam.t 1761. ~

T. Chippendale inv.t et delin.t

Darly. Sculp.t ~

Candle Stands.

T. Chippendale invt. et delin.   Published according to Act of Parliament 1760.

Candle. Stands.

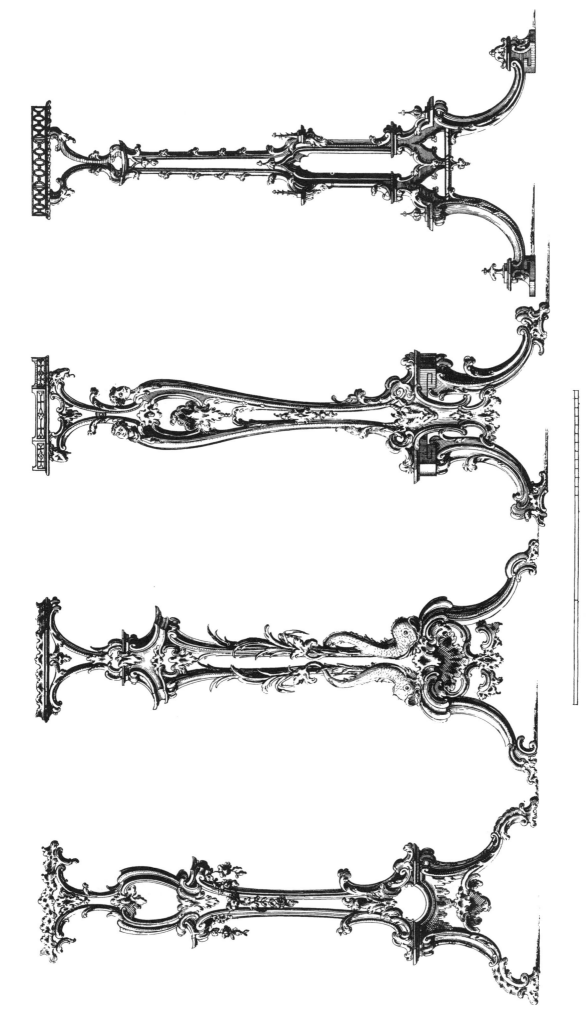

T. Chippendale inv.t et delin.

Publish'd according to Act of Parliament 1760.

Candle Stands.

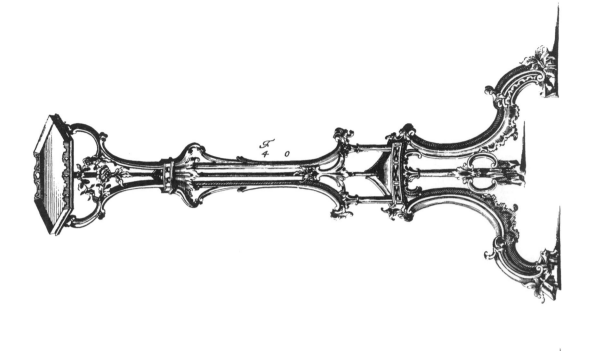

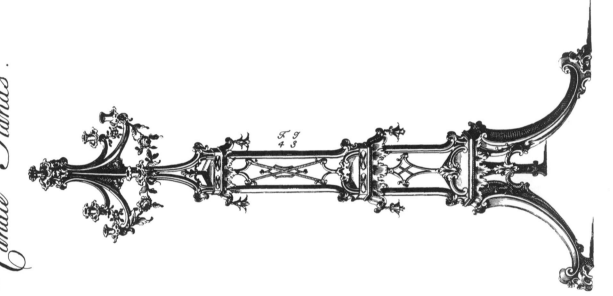

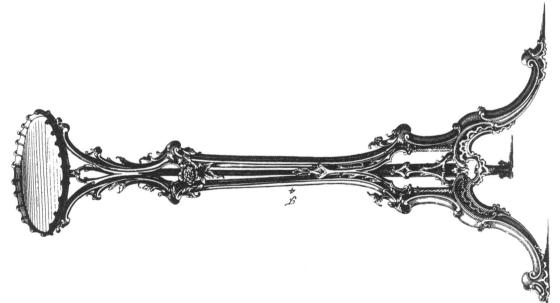

T. Chippendale invt. et del.   Pub.d according to Act of Parliamt. 1753.   J. Darly Sculp.

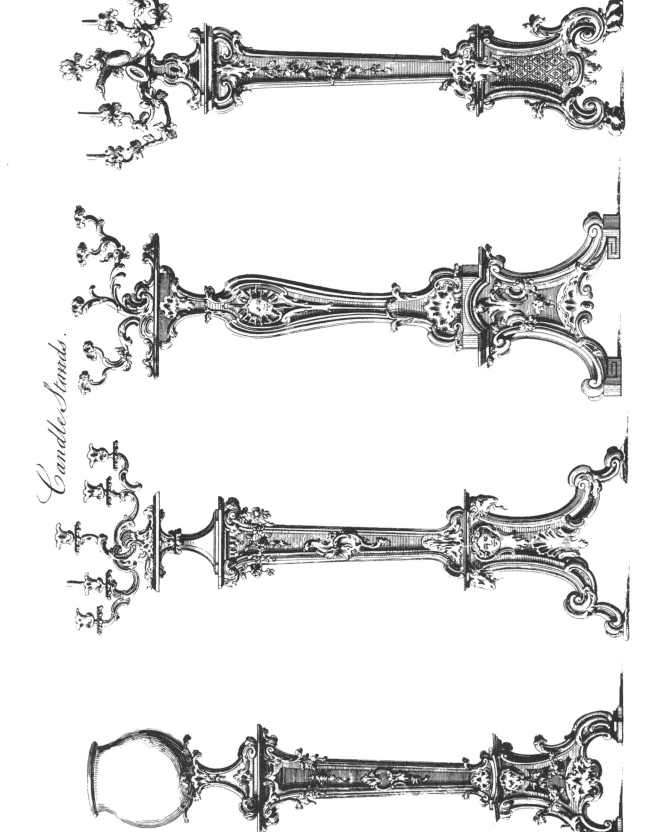

Candle Stands.

Publish'd according to Act of Parliament 1760.

T. Chippendale inv.t et delin.

Terms for Busto's &c.

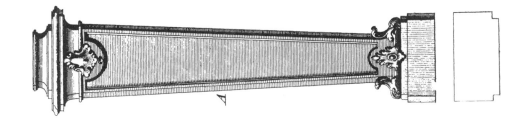

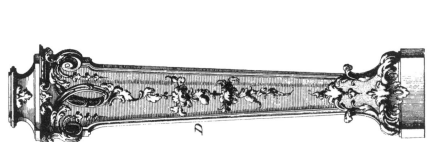

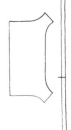

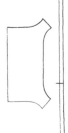

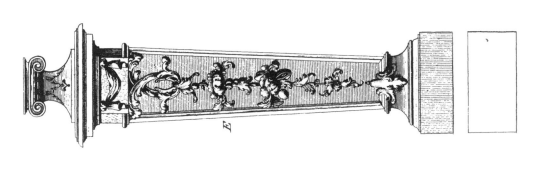

Published according to Act of Parliament 1760.

T. Chippendale inv.t et delin.

Stands for China Jarrs.

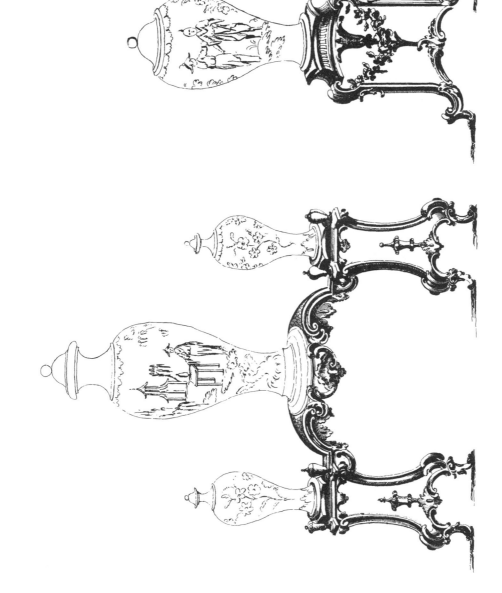

T. Chippendale inv.t et delin.

Publish'd according to Act of Parliament 1760.

W. Foster sculp.

Designs for Pedestals

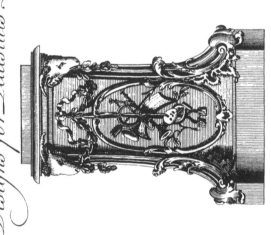

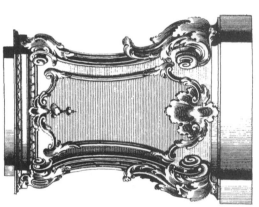

W.ᵐ Foster sculp.

Published according to Act of Parliament 1761.

T. Chippendale invt. et delin.

Cisterns.

T. Chippendale invt. et delin:

Published according to Act of Parliament 1760.

B. Clowes sculp.

T Taylor Sculp

Lanthorns for Halls or Staircases.

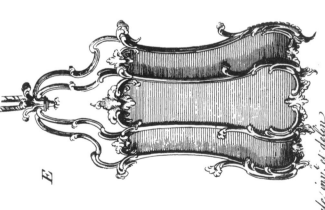

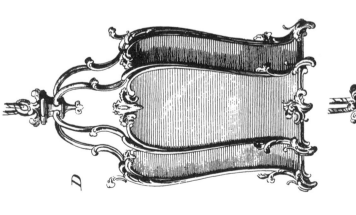

Published according to Act of Parliament 1760.

T: Chippendale invt et delin

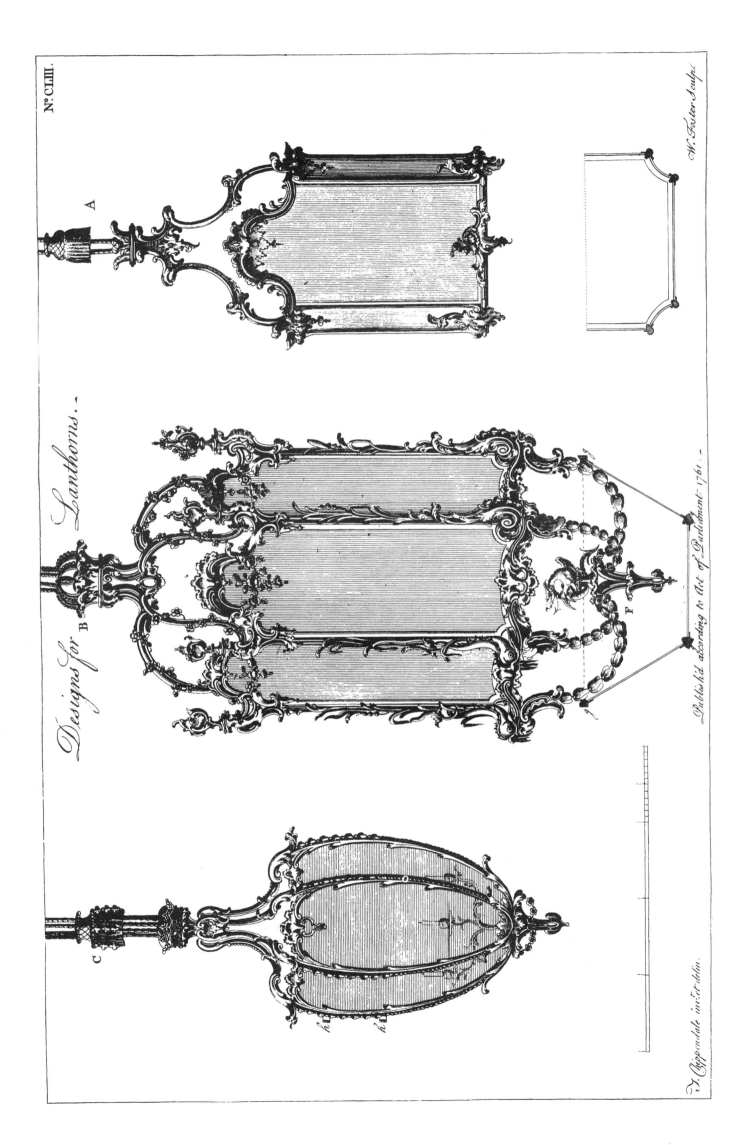

Designs for Lanthorns.

A

B

C

F

J. Chippendale inv. et delin.

Publish'd according to Act of Parliament 1761.

W. Foster Sculp.

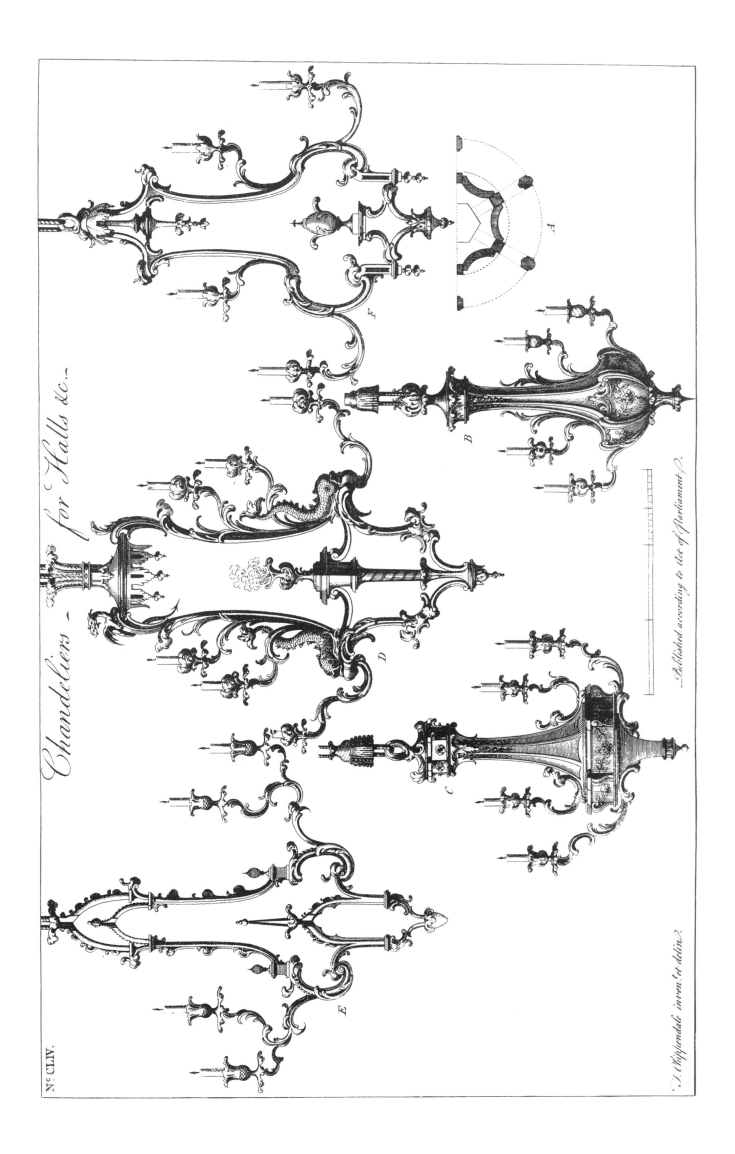

Chandeliers for Halls &c.

Nº CLIV.

Published according to Act of Parliament P.

T. Chippendale invent.t et delin.t

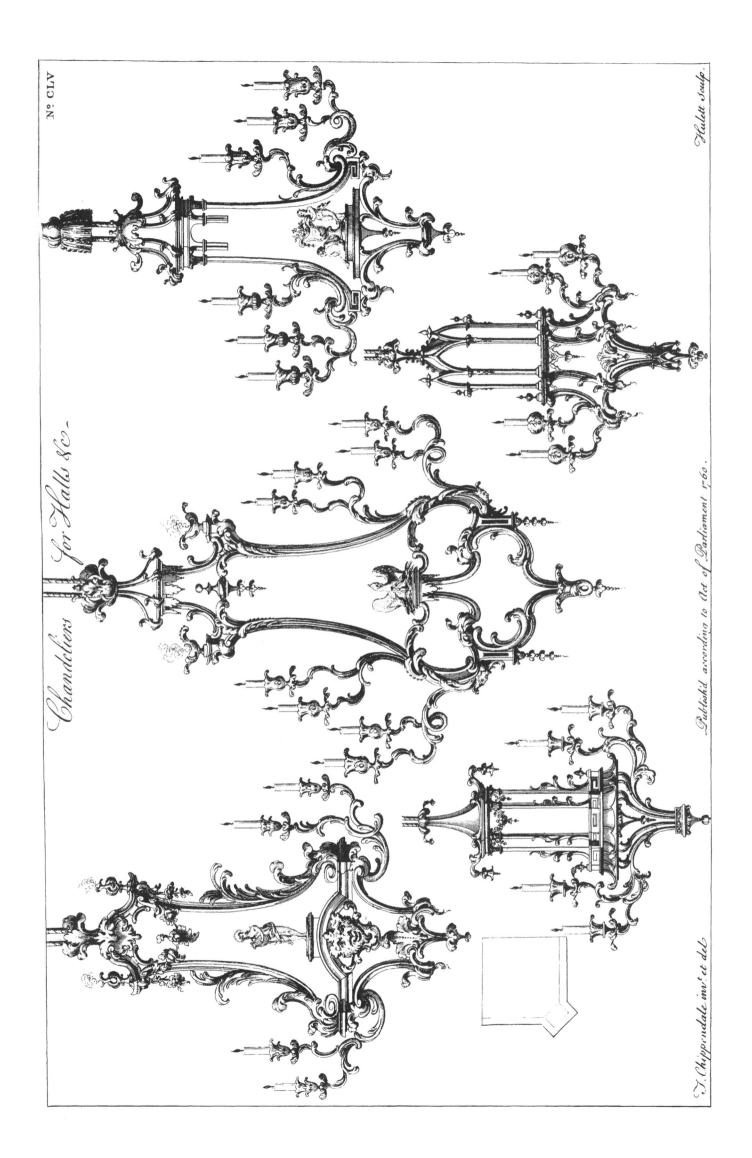

Chandeliers for Halls &c.

T. Chippindale inv.t et del.

Publish'd according to Act of Parliament 1760.

Hulett sculp.

Fire Screens

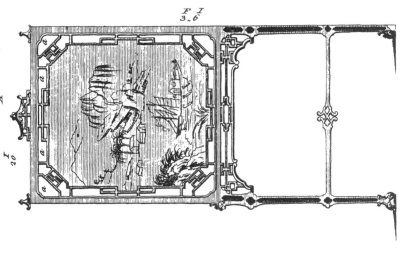

F I
3. 6

A

I
20

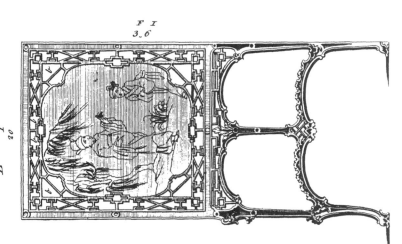

F I
3.. 6

B   I
20

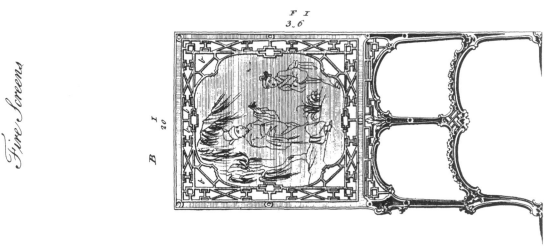

I
18 ½

16

M. Darly Sculp.ˢ

Published according to Act of Parliament

T. Chippendale inv.ᵗ et del.

Fire Screens

A

M.ᵗ Chippordale inv.ᵗ et del.

Published according to Act of Parliament

M. Darly Sculp.ᵗ

Designs for Fire Screens.

T. Chippendale inv.t et delin.   Publish'd according to Act of Parliam.t 1761.   M. Foster Sculp.

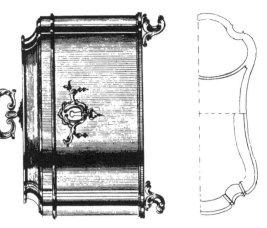

Six Designs of Tea Chests.

M.ʳ Foster Sculp.

Publish'd according to Act Parliament 1762.

T. Chippendale inv.ᵗ et delin.

Brackets for Busts.

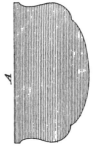

T. Chippendale inv.t et del.

Publish'd according to Act of Parliament.

M. Darly Sculp.

Brackets for Busts.

M. Foster sculp.

Publish'd according to Act of Parliam: 1760

T. Chippendale. invt. et delin.

Brackets for Marble Slabs.

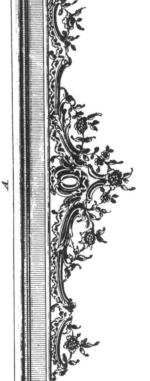

A

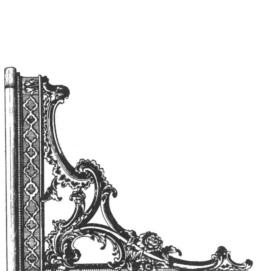

M. Darly Sculp.

Published according to Act of Parliament

T. Chippendale inv.r et del.

Clock Cases.

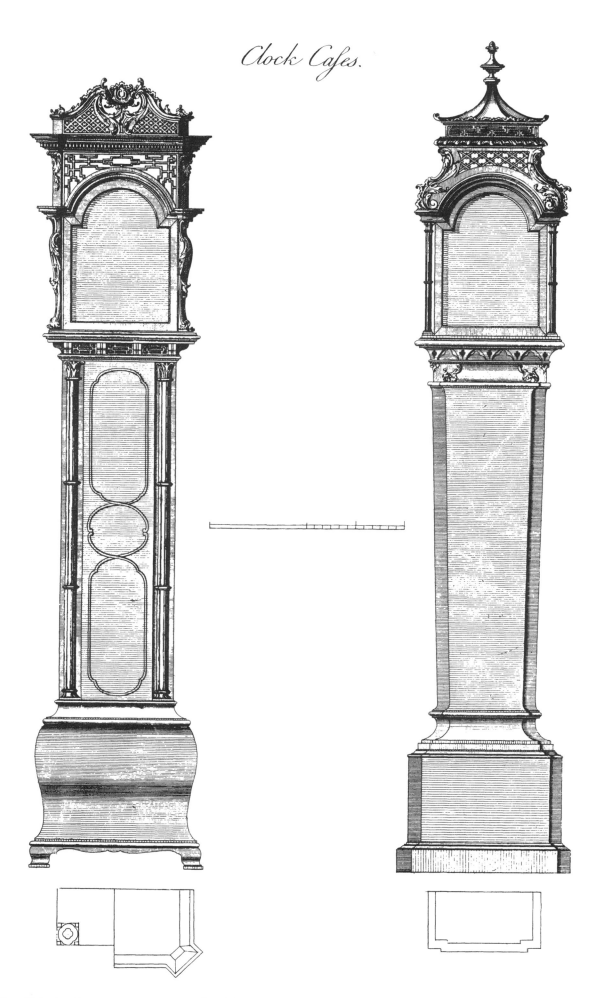

T. Chippendale invt et del.   Publish'd according to Act of Parliament   M. Darly sculp.

Designs for Clock-cases.

J. Chippendale inv. et delin.

Published according to Act of Parliament 1761.

J. Aublett sculp.

Table Clock Cases.

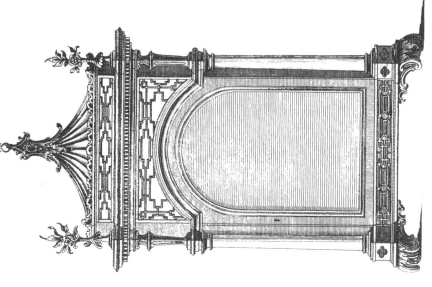

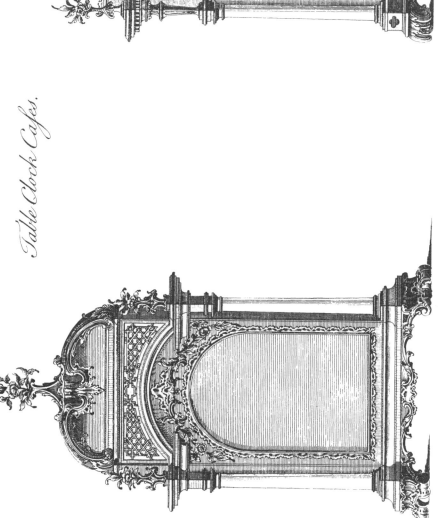

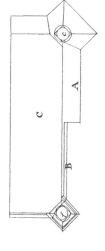

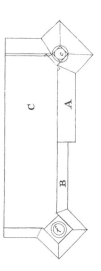

T. Chippendale inv.t et del.

Publish'd according to Act of Parliament

M. Darly sculp.

Designs for Clock-cafes.

G. Chippendale invᵗ et delin.   Publish'd according to Act of Parliamᵗ 1761. —   MDarly sculp.

Designs for Glass Frames.

W. Foster sculp.

Published according to Act of Parliament 1762.

T. Chippendale inv. et delin.

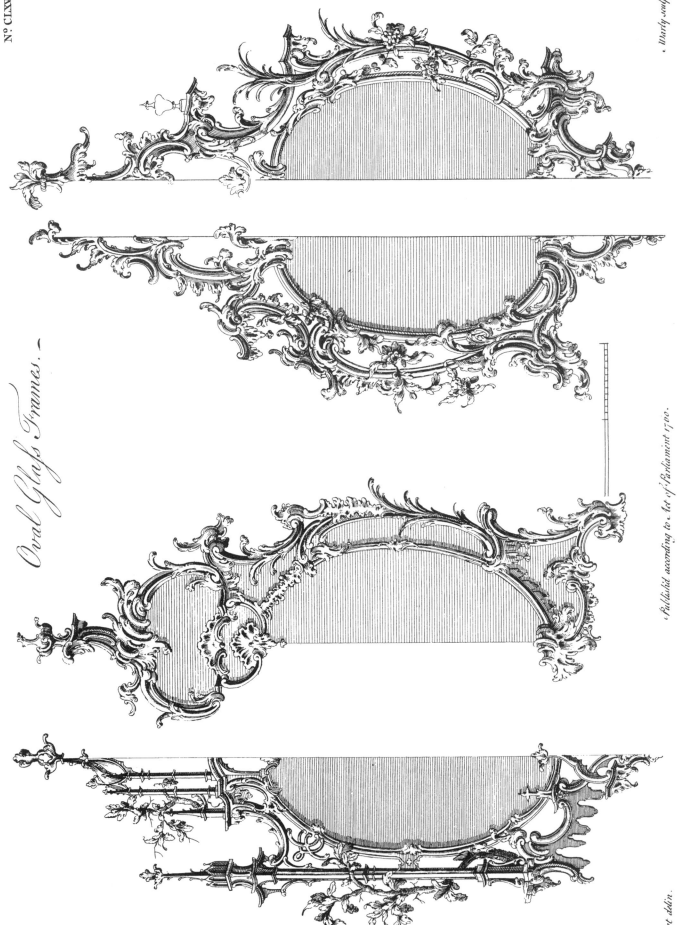

Oval Glass Frames.

Published according to Act of Parliament 1760.

T. Chippendale inv. et delin.

Whorty sculp.

Pier Glass Frame.

T. Chippendale invᵗ et del   Published according to Act of Parliment   M. Dary Sculp.

A Pier Glaſs & Table

T. Chippendale invᵗ et delin   Publish'd according to Act of Parliamᵗ 1760.   B. Clowes Sculp.

Glass Frames

T. Chippendale invt. et delin.   Publish'd according to Act of Parliament 1762.   Isaac Taylor Sculp

Dark Sculp.

Glass Frames.

Publish'd according to Act of Parliament 1760.

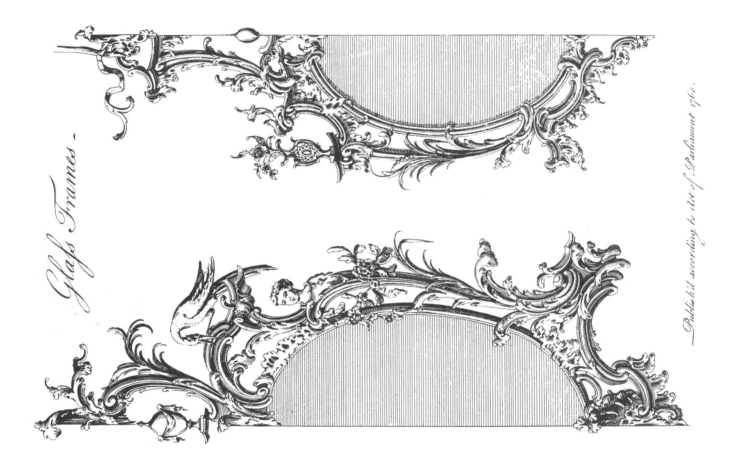

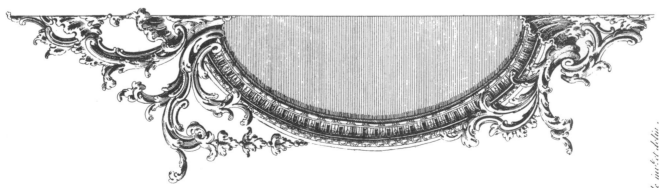

T. Chippendale invt. et delin.

T. Chippendale inv.t et delin ___Publish'd according to Act of Parliam.t 1761. ___W. Foster Sculp __

Pier Glass Frames

I. Chippendale inv.t et del: Publish'd according to Act of Parliament   M. Darly Sculp:

Frames for Marble Slabs.

T. Chippendale inv.t et delin.

Published according to Act of Parliament 1760.

W.r Foster sculp.

Frames for Marble Slabs.

T. Chippendale invt. et delin.   Publish'd according to Act of Parliamt. 1760.   Darly Sculp.

Gerandoles.

T. Chippendale. invt.t delin.t

Publish'd according to Act of Parliament 1760.

Darly Sculp.

Girendoles -

Published according to Act of Parliament 1760 -

B: Clowes Sculp.-

T. Chippendale inv. et delin.

A Design for a Chimney Piece.

T. Chippendale invt et delint.   Publish'd according to Act of Parliamt. 1762.   M Darly Sculp.

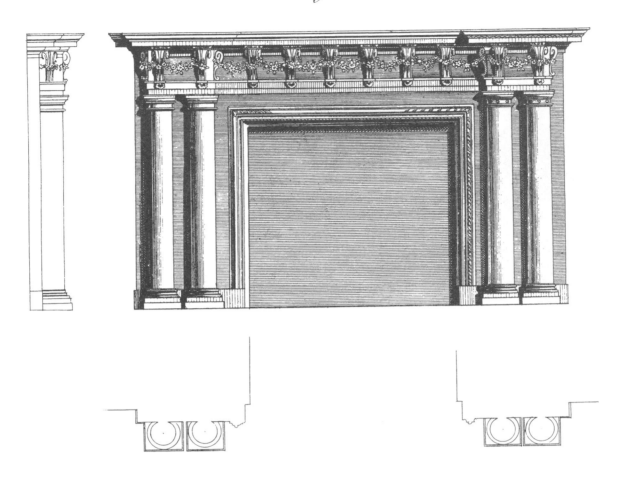

T. Chippendale invt. et delint.
Publish'd according to Act of Parliament 1760.
Darly sculp.

Two Designs for Chimney Pieces.

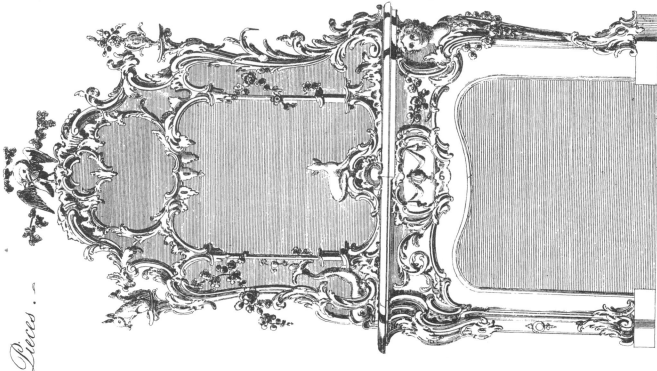

B. Clowes sculp.

Published according to Act of Parliam.t 1761.

T. Chippendale invt & delin.

A Design for a Chimney Piece.

T. Chippendale inv.t et delin.   Published according to Act of Parliamt 1761.   Clowes sculp

Chimney Piece.

T. Chippendale invᵗ et delin.   Publish'd according to Act of Parliament 1761.   W. Foster sculp.

A Design for a Chimney Piece.

J. Chippendale inv.t et delin.   Published according to Act 1761.   M.Darly sculp.

Picture Frame.

T. Chippendale inv.t et delin.   Publish'd according to Act of Parliament 1761.   ADarly sculp

Picture Frame.

T. Chippendale inv.t et delin.   Publish'd according to Act of Parliament 1761.   W. Foster sculp.

A Picture Frame

Inv.t Taylor Sculp.

Published according to Act of Parliament 1762.

T. Chippendale inv.t et delin.

Tabernacle Frames.

Published according to Act of Parliament 1762.

T. Chippendale invt. et delin.

J. Wharly sculp.

Designs for Sheilds.

T. Chippendale inv. et delin.

Published according to Act of Parliament 1761.

J. Darly sculp.

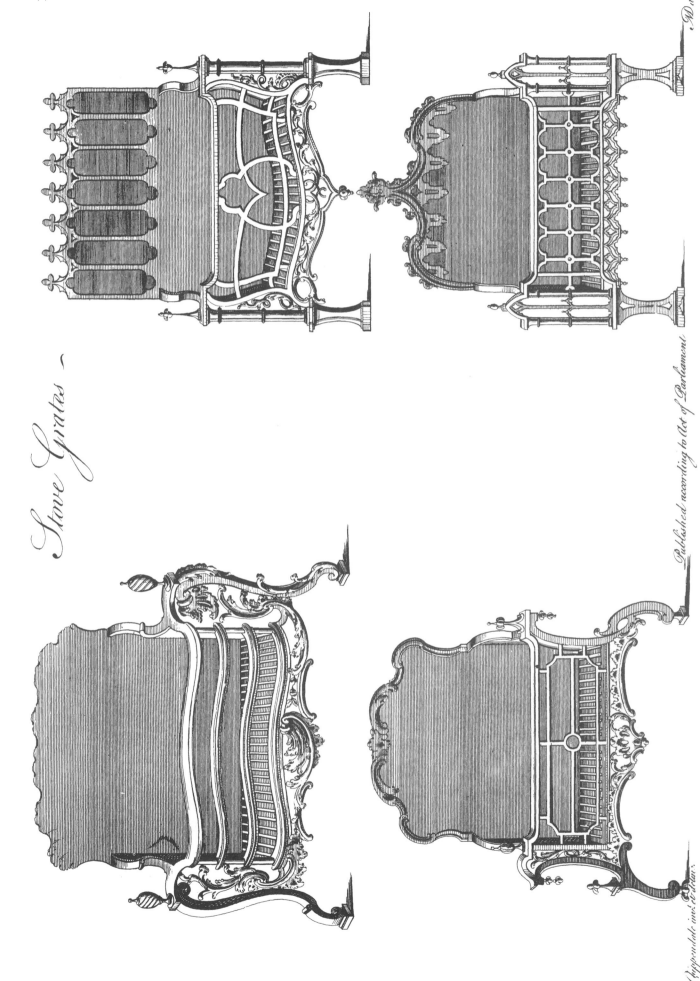

Stove Grates ~

T. Chippendale invt. et delin.

Published according to Act of Parliament

I. Darly Sculp.

Stove Grates.

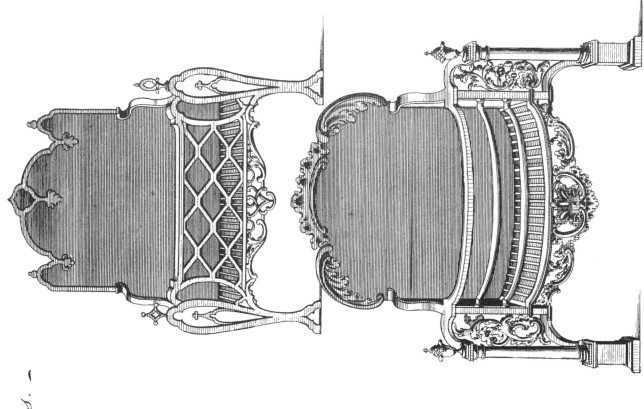

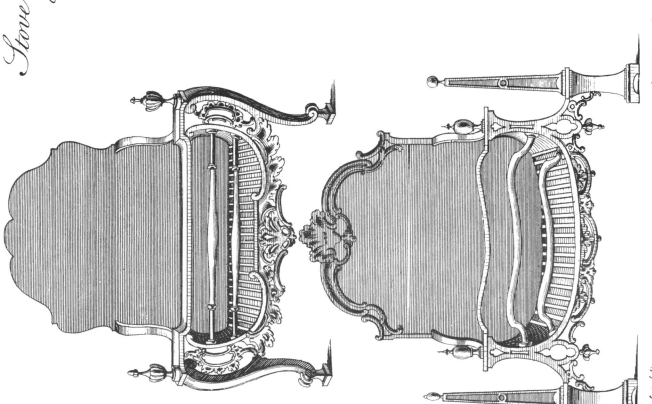

T. Chippendale inv.t et delin.

Published according to e Act of Parliament 1760.

M. Darly sculp.

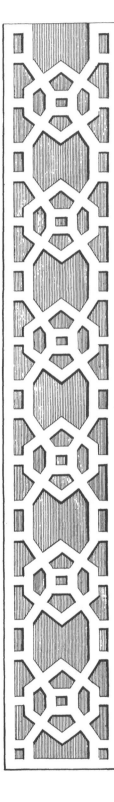

T. Chippendale inv.t et del.

Publish'd according to Act of Parliment.

M. Darly Sculp.

Frets

N.º CXCIII.

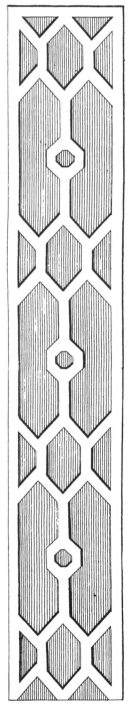
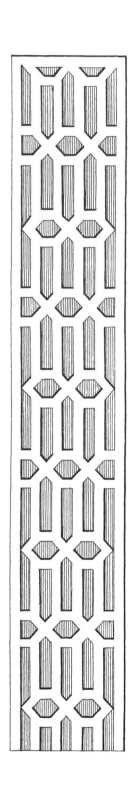

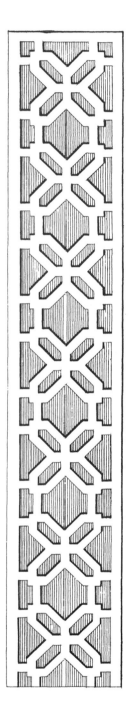

T. Chippendale inv.t et del.

Published according to Act of Parliament

M. Darly Sculp.

T Chippendale invᵗ et delinᵗ   Publish'd according to Act of Parliamᵗ 1761.   B. Clowes Sculp.

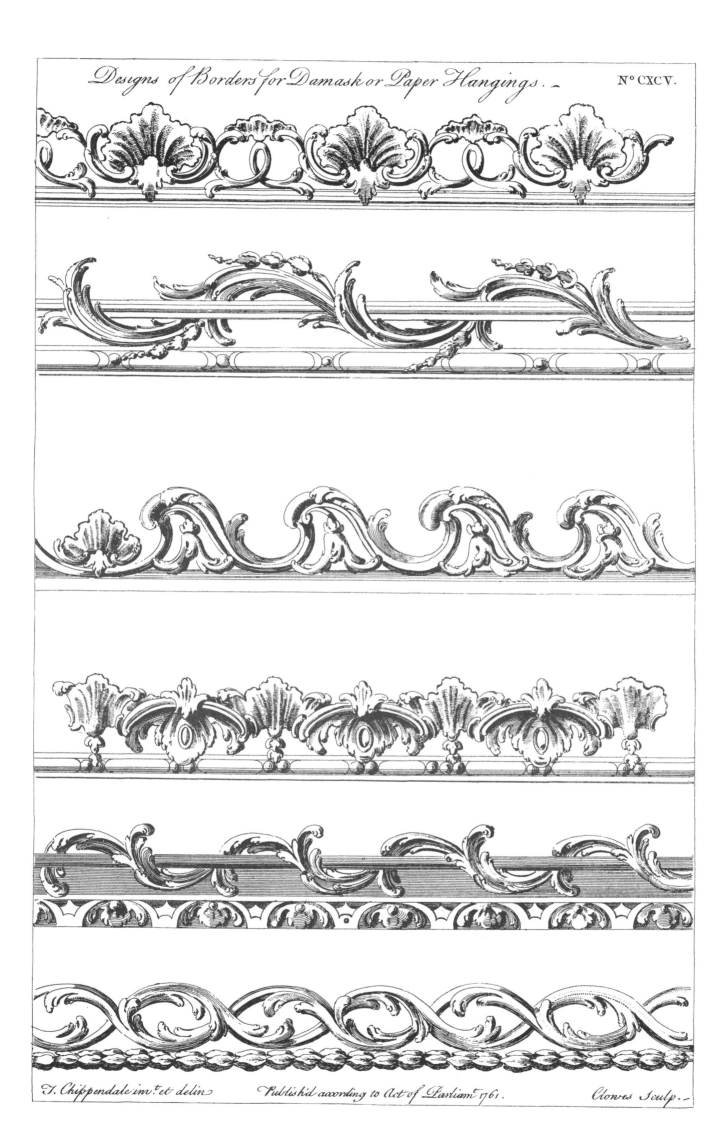

T. Chippendale inv.t et delin   Publish'd according to Act of Parliam.t 1761.   Clowes Sculp.

Gothick frets.

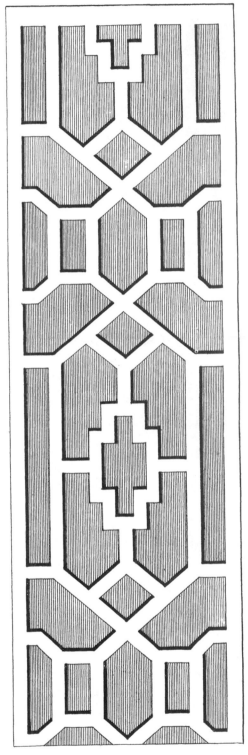

M. Darly Sculp.

Published according to Act of Parliament

T. Chippendale inv.t et del.

Chinese Railing.

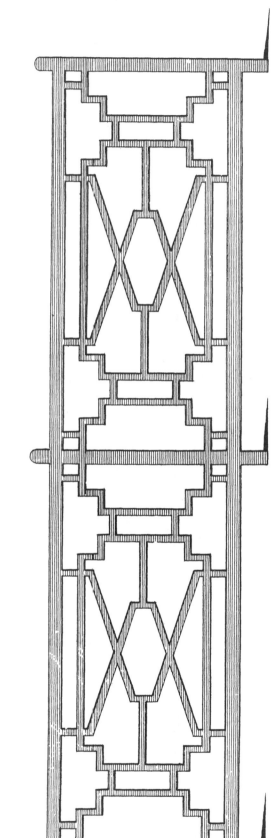

M. Darly Sculp.

Publish'd according to Act of Parliment

T. Chippendale inv.t et del.

N.º CXCVIII

Chinese Railings.

T. Chippendale invr. et del.

M. Darly Sculp.

Published according to Act of Parliament

Designs of Handles for Brass Work.

Publish'd according to Act of Parliament 1761.

T. Chippendale inv.t et delin.

W. Foster sculp.

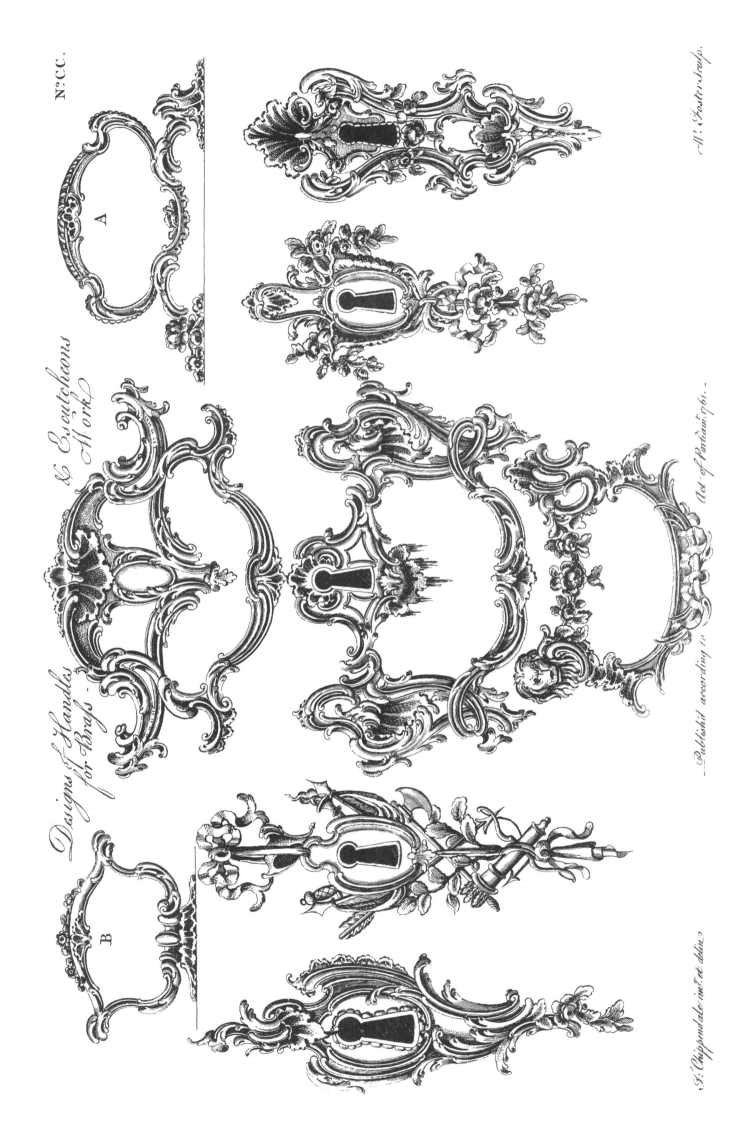

N.º CC.

Designs of Handles & Escutcheons for Brass Work.

A

B

T. Chippendale inv.t et delin.

Published according to Act of Parliament 1761.

M.r Fostirstead.

A Biographical Sketch of

THOMAS CHIPPENDALE

*And a Selection of Photographs
of Chippendale – Type
Furniture*

THOMAS CHIPPENDALE

THOMAS CHIPPENDALE was born in 1718. Some authorities say that he came from the little village of Otley in Yorkshire, England, while others believe that he was born in London and that his father, also a cabinet maker, was already well known for his skill. However, we do know that in 1754, when Chippendale was thirty-six years of age, he published the first edition of *The Gentleman and Cabinet-Maker's Director*.

Of the many books on furniture design which have appeared before or since, this has had by far the greatest influence on English and American Colonial furniture. Its popularity is proved by the fact that a second edition was published the next year and a third seven years later, in 1762. The last one, the edition herein reproduced, had many more plates than the first, and its text was revised to bring it up to date.

Comparatively little is known of Chippendale's life, but it is surmised that he had a thorough apprenticeship in cabinet making after, no doubt, a limited school education. He came from a family in humble circumstances. It is possible that for generations his forebears had been carpenters, joiners and cabinet makers, and it may be that his father and he himself in his early years specialized in carving mirrors and picture frames.

At any rate, Chippendale himself was a master wood carver who was at the same time a master cabinet maker. In addition, he had an inventive mind. This combination, together with his ability to design and more than usual good taste, contributed to his success. His passion for carving gave to English furniture of the mid-eighteenth century its distinct character of carved ornamentation, unassisted, for the most part, by the bronze mountings so much in favor with French designers—in spite of the great popularity of French fashions.

From the meagre facts available concerning Chippendale's life, we know that he was married in London when about thirty years old, and that he had eleven children. During his business career he had two different partners, always, however, remaining himself the most important member of the firm. Just about the time he published the first edition of *The Director,* he became located in St. Martin's Lane, then a fashionable shopping street of London, and his establishment, consisting of three houses, indicated a successful business.

His first wife died in 1772, and five years later he married again, at the age of fifty-nine. This second marriage was to last only two years, for at the end of this time, in 1779, Thomas Chippendale died of tuberculosis. His eldest son, Thomas, carried on the business for some forty years afterwards, dying in 1822 or 1823.

Chippendale's influence spread, not only through the use of his book by fellow craftsmen and wealthy patrons, but also through the furniture which went out of his shop. We have record of only a few of his patrons, but he undoubtedly provided furniture for many fashionable drawing rooms, dining rooms, bedrooms and sometimes entire country mansions and London town houses belonging to the nobility and gentry.

Constantly widening, too, was the influence exerted by the many craftsmen trained in his shop. At one time he had at least twenty-two journeyman cabinet makers working for him, and it may be estimated that the actual number, including apprentices, was at least double that. Workmen trained in his shop went to work for other firms or set up business for themselves, and some no doubt emigrated to this country. It is a fair deduction that some of the cabinet makers who made the famous pieces in Philadelphia in Colonial times had worked in Chippendale's shop.

Chippendale was not only an artist, but at the same time a very practical businessman. He was alert to the fashions of the day and was ready to meet any demands of his customers as long as they met his standard of good design and workmanship.

During his long life as a craftsman, he saw at least five important styles develop and some of them wane, and all of these he either greatly influenced or at least did distinctive work in them. When he began as a journeyman, the early Georgian style was in vogue. Later followed the "French taste," the Chinese style, the Gothic style, and, during the latter half of his working period, the classic style, given its English expression by the London architect, Robert Adam.

The furniture in the early Georgian style was heavy and pompous. Its carved and gilded ornamentation included human and animal faces called masks, lion-heads, carved shells and sturdy pilasters. Animal paws terminated the legs and other supports. Chippendale undoubtedly helped to modify this heavy style, giving it considerable more lightness and grace. Chairs with carved and pierced splats, a cupid's bow top, and the famous claw and ball feet; and pedestal tables with similar feet and carved acanthus leaf decoration are characteristic of him in this period. By the time *The Director* was published this style had been superseded by later ones, so that not many of these decorative motifs were included. We know that Chippendale used the ball and claw foot, for example, but it was not mentioned in the volume.

When the demand for furniture in the French taste began, that is, the rococo style of the court of Louis XV, Chippendale was ready to supply his patrons with pieces carved with extraordinary delicacy, such as his ribbon-back chairs, and other chairs and commodes which followed more closely the foreign style. And when travelers from the Far East began to publish descriptions and pictures of a fascinating and strange land, Chippendale, inspired by these accounts, created what we now call Chinese Chippendale furniture, with its pagoda motifs and delicate fretwork.

During the romantic revival of ancient Gothic motifs for furniture, we find Chippendale making chairs, tables and bookcases with details suggesting tall arched windows, carved pinnacles, trefoil motifs and other features found in cathedrals of the Middle Ages.

The last of the fashions with which Chippendale concerned himself was the classic style, originated about 1760 by Robert Adam. Although it marked a departure from anything which Chippendale had previously done, he undoubtedly was responsible for fine designs in this mode as well as for carrying out Robert Adam's drawings. Much of Chippendale's furniture was made of mahogany, but the master craftsman used other woods, too, including "deal," a kind of pine, for pieces which were to be gilded, lacquered or painted. Under the influence of Robert Adam as well as the fashion for French styles, he made superb pieces with many types of veneers, inlays and sometimes bronze mountings.

Creating elaborate designs for the very wealthy and fashionable people of his day, Chippendale also produced simpler styles of furniture for the less-opulent householder. In descriptions of drawings in his book, he often states that he is willing to simplify the designs. A great cabinet maker, a versatile designer, Chippendale offered this book to the world, as he himself states on the title page, "to improve and refine the present taste," adding that his designs were "suited to the fancy and circumstances of persons in all degrees of life."

Tracing Chippendale furniture back to his workshop is exceedingly difficult, and has been done for only a comparatively few of the many pieces he produced during his lifetime. Like other British cabinet makers of the day, he never signed his products. Some pieces have been authenticated by the original bills of sale, which, with the furniture, remained in the possession of the descendants of the original owners.

For the most part, Chippendale-style pieces which are known to have been made in the eighteenth century are attributed to him because of the similarity of their design to drawings in his book or to work which he is known to have done. It is possible, of course, that some of the furniture in what we call the Chippendale style was made by other cabinet makers who used designs and decorative motifs available to all who had access to Chippendale's book. In furniture which we are certain came from the hand of the master, there is an individuality of design and a vigor and artistry in ornamentation which may be recognized in other pieces.

In the following pages are pictured various styles of Chippendale-type furniture, a few of which may logically be attributed to his workshop.

New York City
April, 1966

N. I. BIENENSTOCK
Editor, *The Furniture World*

PLATE 1. Carved Girandole. A beautiful example of carving. The candleholders
are similar to those included in the designs in Plate CLXXVIII. The ribbon motif is also
suggestive of Chippendale's ribbon-back chairs, as shown in Plate XV. Courtesy
Museum of Fine Arts, Boston.

PLATE 2. Chippendale Armchair. c. 1755. A beautiful specimen of the pierced and carved Chippendale back which corresponds with the design in Plate xiii. Note the vigorous carving on the knees. Courtesy Victoria and Albert Museum, London.

PLATE 3. Ribbon-Back Settee. c. 1755. A remarkable example of Chippendale's
ribbon back, almost identical with a design in Plate xv. The carving on the knee of the
legs is similar to that in Plate xi, and the French scroll foot may be seen in
Plate xx. The Victoria and Albert Museum, which owns this chair and four others in
the same style, has stated that they may be fairly assigned to Chippendale himself.
In this book Chippendale speaks of chairs made from this design as the best he
ever produced. Courtesy Victoria and Albert Museum, London.

PLATE 4. Carved Girandole. Definitely a Chippendale type, this
carved and gilded girandole refutes his contemporaries' criticism that
his designs could not be made into actual furniture. Plate CLXXVIII
shows a design very similar to this one. The original drawing
included candleholders. Courtesy Museum of Fine Arts, Boston.

PLATE 5. Chippendale Carved and Gilded Mirror. c. 1755-60. One of the finest
Chippendale frame designs, combining leaf and 'C' scroll carvings with flower and leaf
drops at the sides. A fine example of rococo taste. (Cf. the designs in Plate CLXVII.)
Courtesy Ginsburg & Levy, Inc., New York.

PLATE 6A. *Chippendale Pierced Splat Chair.*
c. 1755-65. A typical Georgian style in which
Chippendale did a great deal of his work. Note the
angle brackets on the legs. The splat of this chair
corresponds with the design in Plate x. Courtesy
Victoria and Albert Museum, London.

PLATE 6B. *Chippendale English Mahogany Arm-*
chair. c. 1760. This piece has a Gothic back design
and leaf carving, molded arm supports and arms
ending in knuckles. Other Gothic back designs may
be seen in Plate xxv. Courtesy Ginsburg & Levy,
Inc., New York.

PLATE 7A. Chippendale English Mahogany Arm-chair. c. 1760. This piece has an elaborate pierced and leaf carved back, shaped top rail terminating with rolled ears, and a well-shaped arm ending in knuckle scrolls. The front legs are molded with egg and dart edge molding ending in Marlboro feet. Courtesy Ginsburg & Levy, Inc., New York.

PLATE 7B. Chippendale English Mahogany Side Chair in the Chinese Taste. c. 1755-60. One of the many delightful combinations of Oriental and English designs by Chippendale. The carved back design is similar to those pictured in Plate XVI. Courtesy Ginsburg & Levy, Inc., New York.

PLATE 8. Library Breakfront Bookcase. A beautiful piece which exemplifies Chippendale motifs, such as the molding design on the glass doors and the carving on the cupboard doors. From the estate of Lady Sackville-West of Knole, Kent. Courtesy Ginsburg & Levy, Inc., New York.

PLATE 9. Chippendale Mahogany and Gilded Breakfront. c. 1755-60.
This breakfront has an elaborately carved pediment and Greek-key frieze.
The glass molding is similar to the design in Plate XCI.
Courtesy Ginsburg & Levy, Inc., New York.

PLATE 10A (Above). Library Table.
c. 1750-60. This piece shows the
Chippendale style in one of its more
dignified expressions. The flattened
corners, here graced with carved pilasters,
are a motif which Chippendale often used
on cabinet pieces. Many of the details may
be traced to *The Director*. For example,
in Plate LXXXXIII pilasters are shown
in the same general style, with, however,
the single pendant garland replaced by
a rose and leaves. Courtesy Metropolitan
Museum of Art, New York,
Rogers Fund, 1924.

PLATE 10B (Left). Chippendale Gothic
Style Armchair. c. 1770-90. A particularly
fine example of this mode, showing the
cathedral window motifs in the back.
Courtesy Metropolitan Museum of Art,
New York, Bequest of Benjamin Altman,
1913.

PLATE 11A. *Mahogany Folding Card Table. c. 1760-65.* An exceptionally beautiful example of delicate carving. In spite of its fragile air, pieces with carving like this were often quite sturdy. While mainly in the Chippendale Gothic style, as seen in the carved underframing, it is not too archeological in effect as are some other pieces in the Gothic style. Courtesy Metropolitan Museum of Art, New York, Rogers Fund, 1924.

PLATE 11B. *Mahogany Highboy. c. 1765.* The rich carving, as well as excellent proportions of this piece, mark it as an outstanding example of furniture made in Philadelphia in the Chippendale tradition. Courtesy Metropolitan Museum of Art, New York, Kennedy Fund, 1918.

PLATE 12. *Chippendale English Mahogany Splat Chair*. One of a set of six
mahogany side chairs. Many of its details are traceable to designs in *The Director*.
The back suggests an earlier Georgian style. The claw and ball foot terminating the
curved or cabriole leg is not in *The Director*, but is an important feature of many
chair designs which may be traced to this book.

PLATE 13. Chippendale Mahogany Silver Table. c. 1760. A very rare example of an English silver table in the finest taste. The frets on the gallery and pagoda stretcher are the finest known. Courtesy Ginsburg & Levy, Inc., New York.

PLATE 14. Console Table. A beautiful example of the rococo style of carving. Note the slender garlands encircling the cabriole legs; and the scroll leaf foot. The top is dark marble. Formerly the property of Gen. Sir Willoughby Gordon, Bart., of Northcourt, Isle of Wight, 1772-1821. Courtesy Ginsburg & Levy, Inc., New York.

PLATE 15. Console Table. c. 1770. Made in Philadelphia. A superb illustration of
carved cabriole legs and the claw and ball foot. Note the decisive and richly molded
ornamentation of the knees; the claw appears to really grasp the ball. The front of
the table is serpentine shaped, and the top is of marble as is customary. Courtesy
Philadelphia Museum of Art.

PLATE 16. Mahogany Side Chair. c. 1770. This piece was probably made by
Benjamin Randolph of Philadelphia. It is an outstanding example of Chippendale
style which leans toward the French taste as executed in Colonial America. Courtesy
Philadelphia Museum of Art. (Photograph by A. J. Wyatt, Staff Photographer)

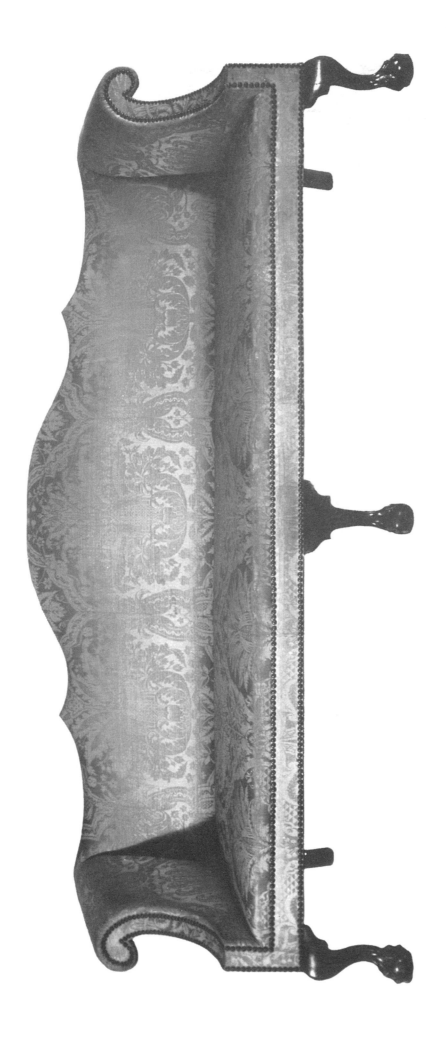

PLATE 17. *Philadelphia Walnut Sofa.* The claw and ball feet, a Chippendale style favorite, are in perfect accord with the graceful lines of the sofa proper. Courtesy Philadelphia Museum of Art.

PLATE 18. Secretary Bookcase. c. 1775. The fine mahogany surfaces provide effective contrast for the carved top of this rare Philadelphia-made piece. Note the Chippendale style of brasses. Courtesy Philadelphia Museum of Art.

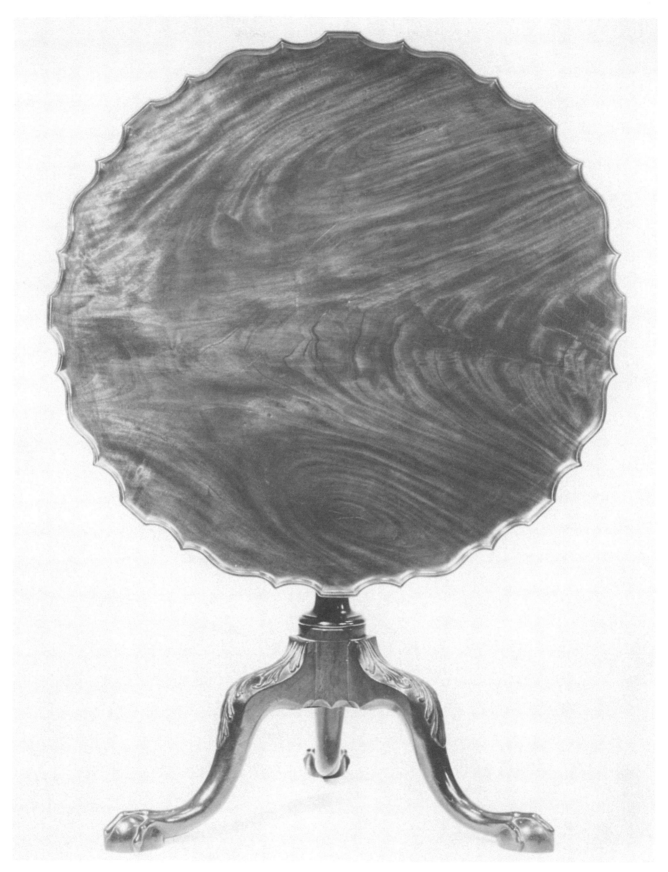

PLATE 19. Philadelphia Chippendale Pie-Crust Table. c. 1780. The carved acanthus
leaves on the legs and the claw and ball foot, as well as the carved edge of the table
cut from the solid top, illustrate the skill of the remarkable group of Philadelphia
cabinet makers. Courtesy Brooklyn Museum.